100 274 202

AUTHOR ..... ILLINGTON ....

TITLE ..... THE FOURTH WINDMILL BOOK
.... OF ONE-ACT PLAYS

THE FOURTH WINDMILL BOOK
OF ONE-ACT PLAYS

The Fourth Windmill Book of One-Act Plays

Seven Plays

by

KENNETH LILLINGTON

With Production Notes

HEINEMANN EDUCATIONAL BOOKS
LONDON

Heinemann Educational Books Ltd
LONDON EDINBURGH MELBOURNE AUCKLAND TORONTO
HONG KONG SINGAPORE KUALA LUMPUR NEW DELHI
NAIROBI JOHANNESBURG LUSAKA IBADAN
KINGSTON

ISBN 0 435 23530 3

Published by
Heinemann Educational Books Ltd
48 Charles Street, London W1X 8AH
Printed Offset Litho and bound in Great Britain by
Cox & Wyman Ltd, London, Fakenham and Reading

Contents

Make Your Play

A Western

CHARACTERS

THE OLD TIMER
MARTHA
THE BARMAN
THE BAD MAN
FIRST SIDEKICK
SECOND SIDEKICK
THE SALOON GIRL
THE SHERIFF
THE LAW MAN
CARD-PLAYERS

MAKE YOUR PLAY

THE SCENE *is a Western saloon, with the bar cutting across the right-hand corner of the stage. In the foreground, extreme left, is a card-table with two players intent upon a game of cards. More tables and pairs of players may be added if the stage is large enough to take them, but they must not obscure the action of the play, to which the card-players pay no attention whatever throughout. The* OLD TIMER *stands in front of the bar, right. He is lined and white-whiskered. He speaks in a terrific Western drawl, ingratiating and full of fake-kindliness.*

OLD TIMER: Howdy, mah friends. Ah shore appreciate yore kinda droppin' in like this. Y'know, thar's far too much bickerin' 'n' grumblin' in this doggone ole world of ours, 'n' it shore would be a better place if more folks kinda dropped in . . . 'n' said howdy . . .

MARTHA (*off; shrill and vituperative*): Git on with it, yew ole fool!

OLD TIMER: Shore will, Martha. Yessir, mah friends, Ah kin remember when even this hyar doggone ole Western drawl ov mine was phoney; but Ah bin doin' it so long now it kinda comes natural . . .

MARTHA (*off*): Fur the Lawd's sake, Ephrim, git on about the gunfight!

OLD TIMER: Ah wuz comin' to that, Martha. Yessir, mah friends, they wuz real gunslicks in them far-off days. They wuz so fast that not even their own reflections in the mirror could keep up with them. They wuz so fast —

MARTHA (*bustling in behind bar, right*): D'yew wanna drive the strangers away with yore gassin', yew ole windbag? Git on about the gunfight at Beaver Creek.

OLD TIMER (*protesting*): Ah wuz jest kinda buildin' up the atmosphere, Martha.

MARTHA: Waal, quit kinda buildin' 'n' start kinda yarnin', or these hyar folks are gonna quit kinda listenin' and start kinda quitt'n'!

OLD TIMER: Yes, ma'am. Waal, folks, it all happened way back, in this hyar same saloon. The place was crowded – folks sittin' around, playin' cards —

THE BARMAN *rises up from behind the bar and begins polishing glasses.*

When, kinda sudden-like, in walk three mean-lookin' jaspers . . . *Brighter lighting. Enter, swaggering, The* BAD MAN *and his* TWO SIDEKICKS. *This entry is prefaced by a salvo of gunshots outside, left.*

The OLD TIMER *withdraws to extreme right and looks on.*

BAD MAN (*slapping money on counter*): Thar's fur yer Widders and Orphans Fund, hombre.

BARMAN: Thank yew kindly, stranger, but we ain't got no widders 'n' orphans in this town.

BAD MAN: No? Jest yew step out 'n' look on the sidewalk. Three whiskeys – 'n' I mean bottles!

FIRST SIDEKICK: An' don't bother about no fancy corkscrew, pard.

SECOND SIDEKICK: Yippee!

Tugs at his gun and fires. A loud bang. He stares at his feet.

(*In a slow drawl*) Waal doggone! Ah've drilled a hole in mah foot!

BAD MAN: Ah've told yew, pardner: yew tie down the holster, not the gun as well.

Enter the SALOON GIRL, *right.*

SALOON GIRL: Hey, yew, Mister Bartender, has mah lovin' Johnny been here?

BARMAN: Try the Public Bar, ma'am.

Exit SALOON GIRL, *after a long, slow, suspicious stare around.*

BAD MAN: Who's she?

BARMAN: A Saloon Girl. Yew guys stayin' long?

BAD MAN: We're jest stayin' till yore Bank opens, hombre!

FIRST SIDEKICK: We figger on robbin' it!

BAD MAN (*rounding on him crossly*): Why doncha keep yore mouth shut? Yew told him now!

FIRST SIDEKICK: Gee, sorry, pard.

BAD MAN: Whadder we gonna do now?

SECOND SIDEKICK: We'll find sumpin!

FIRST SIDEKICK: Shore we will! . . . Ah've got it! (*to Barman*) Say, pard, does a stage coach pass through these hyar parts?

BARMAN: Yessir. Two-thirty, regular. Top o' the Main Street.

BAD MAN: Stage coach?

BARMAN: Yessir. Carries bullion to the Bank, regular.

BAD MAN: Is that so?

BARMAN: Shore is, stranger.

SECOND SIDEKICK: Say, Ah got it – we're figgerin' on —

BAD MAN } Sh–sh!
FIRST SIDEKICK

SECOND SIDEKICK: Oh, yeah! Shore!

Enter the LAW MAN, *right.*

LAW MAN: Jest a minute, stranger. How come yore so interested in our stage coach?

BAD MAN: Waal, s'pose we say we collect stage coach numbers?

LAW MAN: S'pose Ah say yore a liar, stranger.

BAD MAN: 'n' who might yew be?

LAW MAN: Ah'm a Law Man.

BAD MAN: One o' them gun-tot'n' Law Men?

LAW MAN: That's right.

BAD MAN: Let's see yew tote it, Law Man!

They face each other. The TWO SIDEKICKS *scramble behind the bar, with the Barman, and all three duck down behind the counter.*

BAD MAN: Make yore play, stranger.

LAW MAN: After yew. Ah been brought up nice.

BAD MAN: That's mighty civil.

Draws at lightning speed. Roar of gunshots. The LAW MAN *crumples slowly, with considerable dramatic by-play, and the* BAD MAN *raises his barrel to his lips to puff away the smoke. Then he 'freezes' in this attitude, as does everyone else in the saloon, so that there are three*

*heads sticking motionless over the bar, and one of the card-players is
holding a card in mid-air.*

The OLD TIMER *speaks.*

OLD TIMER: Now, 'n' case yew didn't see jest what happened,
we're gonna show yew that gunfight again in slow motion.

MARTHA (*off*): Slow motion warn't invented in them days, yew
ole goat!

OLD TIMER (*in his usual affable drawl*): Kindly keep yore long
sharp weaselly snout outer my business, yew emaciated
crone! (*Snaps his fingers.*) Right, boys!

Action is resumed at a snail's pace. The BAD MAN *and the* LAW MAN
resume former positions and 'draw' very slowly. The LAW MAN'S
gun reaches an aimed position before the BAD MAN'S. *As the latter's
gun is creeping up to 45 degrees to the floor, the* LAW MAN'S *gun is
level. The* FIRST SIDEKICK *looms up over the bar, also of course
in slow motion, clasping a bottle, which he brings down on the law
Man's head. The* LAW MAN *crumples like a deflating concertina as
the* BAD MAN'S *gun comes level. The scene ends in a slow motion version
of the original. It is all done in complete silence.*

OLD TIMER: I hope that helped yew to appreciate the finer
points, folks. (*snaps his fingers.*)

Action is resumed at normal speed. Enter the SHERIFF, *left.*

SHERIFF: Ah heerd shoot'n'.

BARMAN: Shore did, Sheriff. This guy's for Boot Hill.

SHERIFF: That's the kinda thing we gotta put a stop to. Yew do
this, stranger?

BAD MAN: Self defence, Sheriff.

SHERIFF: 'n' how about them guys lyin' around the sidewalk?

BAD MAN: Self defence, Sheriff. Shore is a hostile town.

SHERIFF: What wuz yore quarrel?

FIRST SIDEKICK: Waal, yew see, Sheriff, we wuz jest figgerin'
how we could rob yore stage coach, 'n' this hyar Law Man
comes hornin' in —

BAD MAN: Quiet, stupid! A slip of the tongue, Sheriff!

SHERIFF: Didn't sound like that to me. Ah'm gittin' mighty
suspicious of yew, strangers.

BAD MAN: Yew are?

SHERIFF: Ah shore am. Ah'll be watchin' yew.
BAD MAN: Yew will?
SHERIFF: Ah shore will.
BAD MAN: Is that so?
SHERIFF: It shore is.

Lights fade. They continue talking, but soundlessly. Spotlight on the Old Timer.

OLD TIMER: This hyar western dialogue gits mighty repetitious, folks, so we're gonna skip the follerin' night and mornin', 'n' bring yew back to the Saloon at two-thirty the next afternoon . . .

Black out, to allow BAD MAN, *the* TWO SIDEKICKS, *and the 'corpse' to leave the stage. When the lights go up again, the card-players are carrying on playing, and the* BARMAN *is polishing glasses behind his bar.*

Enter BAD MAN *and* SIDEKICKS, *left.*

BAD MAN (*signalling for whiskey*): Now, yew guys got everything straight?
FIRST SIDEKICK: Shore have, pard. The stage coach draws up outside the Bank 'n' some guys start unloadin' bullion offen it. We shoot them. Thar's a guy ridin' shotgun. We shoot him.
SECOND SIDEKICK: How 'bout thar's some beautiful dame inside the stage coach? Like comin' to teach school?
FIRST SIDEKICK: We shoot her.
BAD MAN: No, we don't. She jest stays thar till the stage coach drives off. Ain't gonna be no woman gits into this act.
SECOND SIDEKICK: How 'bout that thar sneakin' coyote of a Sheriff horns in?
BAD MAN: Yeah. Shore is a problem.
FIRST SIDEKICK: We shoot him.
BAD MAN: Waal, shore. Ah never thought of that.
SECOND SIDEKICK: Better watch them batwing doors.
FIRST SIDEKICK: Shore had. You bend down 'n' tie up yore shoelace, they kin be dangerous.
SECOND SIDEKICK: Ah mean, watch who walks through 'em, stupid!

FIRST SIDEKICK: Oh! O.K.! (*Draws gun and levels it in direction of left.*) Say, here comes someone!

The other two draw and 'cover' the doors. Enter the SHERIFF.

BAD MAN: We got yew covered, Sheriff!

SHERIFF (*calmly*): Not with my draw yew ain't. Drop them guns, boys.

They hesitate.

BARMAN: Best do as he says, fellers.

BAD MAN (*doubtfully*): Yew reckon?

BARMAN: Shore do.

FIRST SIDEKICK: Is he fast?

BARMAN: Shore is.

SECOND SIDEKICK: Kin he shoot a gun outer yore hand?

BARMAN: He kin shoot the slugs back up yore barrel.

FIRST SIDEKICK: Shore is fast. (*Drops his gun.*)

SECOND SIDEKICK: Shore is. (*Drops his gun.*)

BAD MAN: Guess Ah'm euchred, boys. Ah used my last slug killin' that Law Man. (*Drops his gun.*)

SHERIFF: Ah guess yew guys wanna live. (*To Barman*) Git their guns, friend.

BARMAN *emerges and collects guns. One he tucks in his belt; the others he holds in each hand. Then he sticks guns in Sheriff's back.*

BARMAN: O.K., Sheriff, git 'em up, nice and easy.

SHERIFF *raises his hands. They all 'freeze'. The* OLD TIMER *steps forward.*

OLD TIMER: Now, this hyar is one of them unexpected developments without which Western life would tend to git so straightforward as to be positively monotonous. . . .

They unfreeze.

SHERIFF: You'll be sorry for this, son.

BARMAN (*in a high-pitched, overwrought cackle*): Sorry, nothin'. How'd yew like to be a barman 'n' jest stand there polishin' glasses 'n' missing all the shootin' 'n' card-playin' 'n' fun? Ah'm gonna lock yew guys in the back room with this key (*produces an enormous key*) an' Ah'm gonna git me that bullion 'n' ride outer this town 'n' start life anew. Git goin'!

SHERIFF: Which way do we go, son?

BARMAN: Behind the bar 'n' turn left. Yew can't miss it.

They start moving, slowly. A shot from left, off. BARMAN *crumples to the floor. Enter the* SALOON GIRL, *left, gun in hand.*

SHERIFF (*bending over him*): Too bad, son. Yew jest warn't on the right side.

BARMAN: No, they turned me over on my left side, because the bullets hurt me so.

Drops back dead.

SHERIFF (*sententiously, as the* BADMEN *respectfully remove their hats*): Time comes, a man jest has to blaze his own trail. He jest didn't break even. (*To Saloon Girl*) Howdy, ma'am.

SALOON GIRL: Round up the prisoners, Sheriff. They're yours.

SHERIFF: Shore appreciate yore co-operation, ma'am.

BAD MAN: Now jest a minute. How come yew got in on this act?

SALOON GIRL: Ah may be jest a Saloon Girl, mister, but nobody's gonna high-hat me.

BAD MAN: But why'd yew shoot this Barman?

SALOON GIRL: 'cause he wuz impedin' the course of justice.

BAD MAN: 'n' why do yew want justice?

SALOON GIRL: Because . . . (*forgetting her lines*) Because . . .

OLD TIMER: Because yew wuz gonna marry that Law Man this hyar Bad Man shot yesterday.

SALOON GIRL (*brightening*): Yeah, that's right! (*With a sudden accession of theatrical pathos.*) We wuz in love, and he wuz gonna marry me! (*With a change of tone.*) Do yew have his body?

SHERIFF (*courteously*): Ah'm shore sorry, ma'am, but we seem to have mislaid it.

SALOON GIRL: Ah coulda cried over that real purty. Thar's men for yew!

SHERIFF: Allasame, ma'am, Ah guess yew need a man around.

SALOON GIRL: Yew reckon?

SHERIFF: Ah shore do.

SALOON GIRL: Anyone in mind?

SHERIFF: Ah guess Ah ain't much, ma'am, but Ah'd be glad to string along with yew.

SALOON GIRL: Say, yew talk real purty, Sheriff. Ah guess Ah wouldn't mind, at that. Ah shore wouldn't mind, at that.

Sudden, rather intimidating burst of loud, sentimental music, off. SHERIFF *and* SALOON GIRL, *arms round each other, go off left,* 'covering' *the Bad Man and his Sidekicks. The card-players continue playing cards.*

OLD TIMER (*stepping to centre*): Waal, folks, the Ole West wuz hard 'n' mean, but even the roughest, toughest man has got a soft spot in his doggone ole heart if yew care to look for it, 'n' Ah guess we all oughta look real hard for that soft spot, because thar's too much grumblin' 'n' bickerin' in this doggone ole world of ours. . . .

The Curtain begins falling very slowly. MARTHA *bursts in.*

MARTHA (*screaming with vexation*): Yew mangy ole dingo, yew *still* ain't told 'em about the Gun Fight at Beaver Creek! Don't lower the curtain yet, fellers! . . . Don't lower the curtain, yew lousy coyotes! Don't go, strangers! (*The curtain closes round her.*) Stay around! Ah'll tell yew! Aw, for Pete's sake . . .!

The CURTAIN *closes before her face.*

Bring Out Your Dead

A Hospital Drama

CHARACTERS

PETER MALADY, *a young surgeon*
MAURICE MANDRAKE, *an old surgeon*
NURSE POPPET
CUTHBERT SMIRKE, *a young doctor*
ANAESTHETIST
SISTER AGATHA HAGBIRD
WALLABY, *an Australian doctor*
FOBIA, *a coloured doctor*
PATIENT (etherized on table)

THE SCENE *is an operating theatre in a hospital. It may be furnished at the producer's discretion, the only essential requirement being the operating-table, centre, which supports an unconscious patient. Young* MR MALADY *is operating. At the head of the table, right, are the Anaesthetist and Nurse Poppet, an adorable blonde. Also present are Mr Mandrake and Dr Smirke.*

MALADY: Forceps.

NURSE: Forceps. (*Hands them up.*)

MALADY: Clip.

NURSE: Clip. (*Hands it up.*)

MANDRAKE (*in a tone of heavy sarcasm*): Just what are you doing, Malady?

MALADY (*stiffly*): My best, sir.

MANDRAKE: To what end?

MALADY: To save this man's life.

MANDRAKE: I should never have guessed.

MALADY (*suppressing his resentment*): Needle.

NURSE: Needle.

MALADY: Thread.

NURSE: Thread.

MALADY: Thimble.

NURSE: Thimble.

   MALADY *holds up needle and thread in his fingers and squints at them.*

SMIRKE (*young, chirpy and rather tactless*): Actually I find it better to bring the thread to the needle, old boy.

MALADY (*grimly*): Thanks.

   He fumbles under the sardonic eye of Mandrake, but begins sewing.

MANDRAKE: Ah, we're off. One, out. In, out. (MALADY *whips*

back his finger with an intake of breath.) Ah, dear me. We've caught a crab.

MALADY (*smouldering with rage*): The thread slipped out.

MANDRAKE: You should have knotted it, shouldn't you? (*To anaesthetist*) How is he?

ANAESTHETIST (*a laconic type*): Coping.

MANDRAKE: Marvellous, how they cling to life. (MALADY *is now stitching methodically.*) Ah, that's neat, Malady. No one will undo that in a hurry.

MALADY *straightens up, sighs, wipes his forehead and begins pulling off his gloves.*

But one moment . Where have you left your thimble?

MALADY *starts wildly, bends down to peer at the patient, looks frantically about for a few moments.*

MALADY (*in despair*): Oh, no!

MANDRAKE: I fear so.

MALADY (*brokenly, to Nurse*): Bodkin.

MANDRAKE (*with sudden impatience*): Ah, for Heaven's sake, let me do it!

His hands flash over the body; he draws out several yards of thread, dips in, and fishes out the thimble.

There! (*To Nurse*) Put this where it can't gum up the works! Now, Malady, watch! (*He bends over: his elbow makes undulating movements for a few seconds.*) There! That's how it should be done! Mind you, he doesn't look too good. A bit like a war-time graveyard from the air. But whose fault is that? Right, gentlemen! Wheel him away before Malady dismantles him completely!

He strides out, pulling off gloves, mask, and coat, and throwing them down contemptuously for the others to collect.

SMIRKE (*consolingly, as the operating-table is wheeled out*): Don't worry, old boy. His bark's worse than his bite.

Exeunt everyone except Malady and Nurse Poppet. MALADY *sinks into a chair and clasps his head in his hands.* NURSE POPPET *touches his hand, timidly.*

MALADY (*wearily*): What is it, Nurse Poppet?

NURSE: It's—it's just that I can't bear to see you so upset, Mr Malady.

MALADY (*bitterly*): I'm a failure.

NURSE: No, no, you're not! Mr Mandrake's hard on everyone! Sarcastic old thing!

MALADY (*soberly*): He's a great surgeon.

NURSE: He thinks he is.

MALADY: No, he's great. His needlework is magnificent.

NURSE: Well, I think *you're* great.

MALADY: Don't be silly. (*With awakened interest.*) You do!

NURSE (*softly*): I think you're the greatest.

MALADY: Go on. I like flattery.

NURSE: I would, if I had time.

MALADY: Are you off duty, tonight?

NURSE: Yes.

MALADY: How about eight o'clock at 'The Stomach Pump'?

NURSE: Love to.

> *He pulls her on to his knee. Enter* SISTER HAGBIRD.

Oh! Sister Hagbird! (*Jumps up in confusion.*)

SISTER (*harshly*): Nurse Poppet! What exactly are you doing just now?

NURSE: I'm – I'm attending an operation, Sister.

SISTER: Oh? Which of you is the patient?

NURSE: It's finished now, Sister.

SISTER: It is indeed. Return to Ward immediately. Take the empty crates from the boxroom and leave them by the lift for the porter.

NURSE: Very good, Sister. (*Turns to go.*)

SISTER: Wait. (*Imperiously*) Screens, nurse.

> NURSE POPPET *fetches two screens and fits them round Malady and the Sister, so that they form three sides, open to the audience. Exit* NURSE.

SISTER (*in a low, urgent voice*): Peter, why have you been avoiding me?

MALADY: I haven't, Agatha. I've just been busy.

SISTER: That doesn't explain your clattering down the fire escape whenever I enter a room. What's wrong, Peter? Don't I count any more?

MALADY (*insincerely*): Oh, yes. Of course you do.

SISTER: Prove it, then. Take me out tonight. How about eight o'clock at 'The Stomach Pump'?

MALADY: Well, no – not actually tonight, I can't —

SISTER: I see.

MALADY: Agatha —

SISTER: Don't apologize.

MALADY: Look here – I must be going.

SISTER: Don't let me keep you.

MALADY: Oh —! (*Exit*)

> SISTER HAGBIRD *stands still for a few moments, dabbing at her eyes. Enter* DR SMIRKE, *right.*

SMIRKE (*peering round screen*): What's this, an attack of agoraphobia?

SISTER: *Agatha*phobia, you mean. Peter's got it badly.

SMIRKE: Well, I should step out of there, quick. You look daft. I say, can I read you a bit of my new poem?

SISTER: No.

SMIRKE: It's called, 'The Love Song of J. Benjamin Killdog'. It begins:

> Let us go, then, you and I,
> When the patient's etherized upon a table
> Like an evening, spread out against the sky.

SISTER: It sounds familiar, somehow. Cuthbert, do go away.

SMIRKE: Oh, all right. (*Exit.*)

> SISTER HAGBIRD *begins wearily to replace the screens. Enter* MANDRAKE, *left.*

MANDRAKE: Ah, Agatha! Are you free tonight?

SISTER (*busy with the screens*): Yes, I suppose so.

MANDRAKE: Capital. How about eight o'clock at 'The Stomach Pump'?

SISTER (*finishing business with screens*): No, Maurice.

MANDRAKE: Oh, but —

SISTER (*facing him*): *No,* Maurice.

MANDRAKE: Any special reason?

SISTER: Yes. You repel me.

MANDRAKE: But can't you see what I have to offer you?

SISTER (*shuddering*): I can imagine it.

MANDRAKE: Come now, wouldn't it be better to be Mrs Mandrake than Sister Hagbird?

SISTER: Frankly, I don't think there's much in it.

MANDRAKE (*angrily*): Oh, very well. *Stay* desiccated, then.

Exit in dudgeon, right. Enter DR WALLABY *and* DR FOBIA, *a coloured doctor of indeterminate race.*

WALLABY: And this is the operating theatre, sport. It's not half bad by lousy Pommie standards.

FOBIA (*in a sing-song voice*): Fascinating. And this is a patient, awaiting plastic surgery, it stands to reason?

WALLABY: No, no, sport. This is Sister Hagbird.

FOBIA: Ah, pardon me, I shouldn't wonder.

WALLABY (*clumping her on the back*): Good on you, Haggie! This is Dr Fobia. He's studying our methods.

SISTER (*wincing*): How do you do.

FOBIA: Very well, thank you, apart from nausea at English food. Sister Haggie, I am profoundly impressed at your astounding hospital, no?

SISTER: No?

FOBIA: Oh yes, I regretfully state. In my country, the hospitals are more limited.

SISTER: Really?

FOBIA: Alas, yes. Our hospitals are merely for the care of the sick. Yours cater also for the full social life.

SISTER: Oh, they certainly do. Mind you, not everyone gets sociable.

FOBIA: Ah, then, what do you do when the social life gets flat, I have no doubt?

SISTER: Oh, then we have an operation.

FOBIA: That is of the most fascinating. Tell me: there is a local hostelry, much frequented by the medical profession: it is called 'The Stomach Pump', is it not?

SISTER: Yes.

FOBIA: At what hour is the dining, I am ashamed to say?

SISTER: Eight o'clock.

FOBIA: Would it be permitted to dine there with one of the nursing staff, as for instance yourself, I beg to differ?

SISTER: Why yes, certainly!

FOBIA: That is of the most exhilarating. It is not, in point of fact, yourself, Sister Haggie, but a certain young nurse of the most delectable: she is named Nurse Poppet, I frankly admit.

SISTER: Oh, is she. Well, you'll have to get in the queue for that one.

FOBIA (*puzzled*): Please?

SISTER: Don't mention it.

A long A-a-a-a-h!! off, followed by a tremendous crash; shouts, shrieks, ringing of bells, whistles, etc.

FOBIA: Ah, this will be the operation!

WALLABY: Sounds like you're too right, sport.

SISTER: Good gracious, what's happened?

Enter DR SMIRKE.

SMIRKE: By gosh, did you hear that? Not with a whimper but a bang, eh?

SISTER: Cuthbert, what's happened?

SMIRKE: It's old Mandrake. He's fallen down the lift shaft!

Enter NURSE POPPET.

NURSE: Oh, Sister, Mr Mandrake's killed himself, and it's my fault!

SISTER: Steady, now. How can that be?

NURSE: Those crates! I left them by the lift and he fell over them. The gates were open —

SMIRKE: All glassy-eyed, he was. As if he were sleepwalking. He walked straight at the lift gates. I watched him, fascinated. He didn't stop. He fell over the crates and pitched down the shaft head first.

NURSE (*tearfully*): You see?

SISTER: No, no, nurse. You mustn't blame yourself. It was my fault.

NURSE: Oh, no —

SISTER: Yes. It was something I said to him. That was why he was so distracted. Oh, I'll never forgive myself!

Enter MALADY, *the brilliant surgeon arriving in the crisis.*

NURSE: But the crates — it was my fault.

SISTER: No, no; mine.

MALADY (*sternly*): All right, this is no time for your masochistic wallowings. Shut up, both of you. They're bringing him in.

MANDRAKE, *groaning weakly, is wheeled in. Anaesthetist follows.*

NURSE (*to Sister*): How masterful he is!

MALADY (*inspecting the body*): H'm. Yes. (*To Smirke*) What's your opinion, Cuthbert?

SMIRKE: Prolapsed fracture of the trachea, collateral bruising, dorsal contusion and abrasions, anthrax of the thorax, and profuse sanguinary effusion from the proboscis. Also a dirty great iron spike is rammed right through his chest.

MALADY: Good Man. My God, what a mess!

SMIRKE: Will you operate, Peter?

MALADY: No option. That spike must come out.

SISTER (*to Nurse Poppet*): And this is the boy they said couldn't open a can of beans!

WALLABY: Shall I inject him, cobber? I've brought some fair dinkum dope up from Down Under.

MALADY (*brusquely*): No. Keep it for calming frenzied aborigines.

WALLABY (*muttering*): Stuffy boiled-shirt Pommie prejudice!

MALADY (*to Anaesthetist*): Are you ready? (ANAESTHETIST *nods.*) Let's get started, then. (MANDRAKE *groans.*)

A large instrument surprisingly like a cylindrical vacuum cleaner is wheeled in by orderlies. It is placed near the head of Mandrake. A tube from it is pushed under his head and it is switched on. While the roar lasts, the cast assembles round the body; ANAESTHETIST *at the head, right;* NURSE POPPET *next to him;* MALADY *next to her, centre;* SMIRKE *next and* WALLABY *next, by his feet, left.* SISTER HAGBIRD *and* DR FOBIA *look on left, a little apart from the others.*

MALADY (*as the roar is switched off*): How is he?

ANAESTHETIST: Dodgy.

MALADY: Will he cope?

ANAESTHETIST: Maybe.

MALADY: Like that?

ANAESTHETIST: Uh-huh.

MALADY: Oh, well. Lancet.

NURSE: Lancet. (*Hands it up.*)

SISTER (*to Fobia*): One thing about an operation, it does come in handy when you run out of dialogue.

SMIRKE: Peter.

MALADY: M'm?

SMIRKE: His teeth.

MALADY: Teeth?

SMIRKE: Better take them out. Don't want him to swallow them.

MALADY: Good point, Cuthbert. Thanks. (*He removes a large set of false teeth from Mandrake and holds it aloft.*) No, he wouldn't like that, at all.

NURSE: I'll take them, Mr Malady.

MALADY: Yes — (*Suddenly, before she can take them*) Tweezers, nurse. *Tweezers!*

NURSE (*in panic*): There aren't any.

MALADY: Get some. Get some! (*She runs out.*) My God, hurry, hurry, hurry, girl. This is touch and go.

ANAESTHETIST: Mr Malady, it's going to be dangerous to keep him under any longer.

MALADY: I know. (*Re-enter Nurse Poppet.*) Come on, come on. Wherever have you been?

NURSE (*hurt*): I was as quick as possible, Mr Malady.

MALADY: All right, all right. Don't stand there apologizing. (*He fiddles authoritatively for a few moments.*) Got it! By Timothy, got it! (*Holds up an iron spike about twelve inches long.*) Needle, nurse.

NURSE: Needle.

MALADY (*still irritable*): And the rest. Come on, come on. (*He sews furiously for a few moments.*) Phew! I'm finished – the question is, is he finished too?

ANAESTHETIST: I don't like the look of him.

MALADY: Well, no one does. But is he alive?

ANAESTHETIST: Ah! His ears are twitching.

SMIRKE: Might be a trick of the wind.

MALADY: Come, come, this isn't an open-air theatre.

SMIRKE: I didn't mean open-air wind. Ah! he's moving, definitely.

MALADY: Yes, he's alive. Phew!

NURSE: Oh, Mr Malady, you're marvellous!

SMIRKE: Congratulations, Peter.

MALADY: Thanks, Cuthbert.

WALLABY: Good on you, sport.

MALADY: Thanks, old man. Sorry I was a bit sharp just now.

WALLABY (*shaking hands heroically*): Forget it.

MALADY: Nurse Poppet – sorry I barked. Forgive me?

NURSE: Forgive you —! Oh, I wish we could do this every day!

ANAESTHETIST: Psst! He's coming round.

 MANDRAKE *groans and sits up, slowly and weakly.*

MANDRAKE: Why are you lot all staring at me? (*moves incautiously.*) Ouch!

MALADY: Steady, sir.

MANDRAKE: What —? Oh Lord, I remember: the lift shaft – fell down it – good Lord, the odds are I should have broken my neck. *Did* I break my neck?

MALADY: No, but there *were* a few complications, sir.

SISTER: Mr Malady operated, Maurice.

NURSE (*ecstatically*): With his bony, sensitive hands!

MANDRAKE: Operated?

ALL: Yes!

MANDRAKE: Saved my life?

ALL: Yes!

MANDRAKE (*calmly*): The devil he did. I always knew he had it in him.

ALL (*roguishly*): Oooh!!

MANDRAKE: Oh yes, I did. In my sardonic old heart I've always had a soft spot for the boy. Well done, Malady.

MALADY: Thank you, sir.

MANDRAKE: What's this? (*Feeling his mouth.*) Ah, you've taken my teeth out, have you?

MALADY: I thought it a wise precaution, sir.

MANDRAKE: Very sound, my boy. Very sound. But let's have 'em back now.

MALADY: Of course, sir. Teeth, nurse.

NURSE: Tee — Oh, no. I haven't got them, Mr Malady.

MALADY: But I gave them to you!

NURSE: No, Mr Malady. You began to, then you sent me out for the tweezers. I never took them.

SMIRKE: That's right, Peter.

MALADY: Then where are they?

MANDRAKE (*irately*): Yes, where are they? Stop messing about and give them to me!

MALADY: Sir – I'm terribly sorry – they seem to have disappeared.

MANDRAKE: Good Heavens, man, they can't have gone far, can they? You've been standing over me all the time — (*He stops in horror.*) Oh, *no!* (*He begins patting himself all over, at first gingerly, then with mounting vigour and fury.*) You couldn't have! (*Wildly.*) What am I saying? Couldn't have? Of course you could! You always do, don't you? Always leave a little something behind! Tell me, is it superstition or just your idea of etiquette? (*In a paroxysm of fury.*) Why, you – *imbecile* – you – *lunatic* —

SISTER: Control yourself. You'll burst your stitches.

SMIRKE (*aside to Wallaby*): Dare I say, I knew he had it in him?

ANAESTHETIST: The psychiatric boys'd be interested in this. They'd say you'd got a Trojan Horse complex, Malady.

MANDRAKE: Trojan Horse —! (*Gibbering.*) Get out! Get out, the lot of you!

General pandemonium.

ANAESTHETIST ⎤   But we can't —
NURSE   ⎬ (*together*): Oh please, Mr Mandrake —
MALADY   ⎦   I can't just forget about it —

MANDRAKE (*roaring*): Go on, get out! I'll do it myself! Yes, I will! I will not be made a waste-bin of! Give me a local and GET OUT!!

WALLABY (*eagerly*): I've got some dinkum dope —

MANDRAKE: Take it out with this other dinkum dope (*pointing to Malady*) and throw it into the incinerator. GET OUT, Get — *The* ANAESTHETIST *quietly cracks him on the head with a small ivory hammer. He drops back, senseless.*

ANAESTHETIST: Only way. He can't take another lot of gas.

Now, Mr Malady: we'd better get cracking again. And fasten down all moveable objects.

MALADY (*shaken and nerveless*): Yes. Yes, all right.

Everyone, except Dr Fobia and Sister Hagbird, falls upon the table and shoves it as far back as it will go. They surround it, hiding it from the audience. All we can see is a flurry of arms and elbows.

SISTER (*upstage, centre*): Well, Dr Fobia: now you've seen something of our methods!

FOBIA: And I am tremendously impressed, I hate to think; but far from satisfied, Sister Haggie.

SISTER: No?

FOBIA: No. There so many loose ends. I wish to know: will Mr Mandrake ever forgive Mr Malady? Who will eventually marry the succulent Nurse Poppet? How does Dr Smirke's poem end? Will you continue to spurn Mr Mandrake? When shall all of us meet at eight o'clock at 'The Stomach Pump', I have no doubt?

SISTER: My dear Dr Fobia, you want to know too much all at once. You can't possibly hope to settle all that in a single instalment. This —

The curtain begins to fall

– goes on for *years*. . . .

CURTAIN

I'll Ring For More Toast

A Comedy of the 'Thirties

CHARACTERS

MRS SWAYNE
LADY FOOTLE
RUBBISH, *a butler*
CHARLES
BETTY
DADDY
FIRST RED
SECOND RED

I'LL RING FOR MORE TOAST

SCENE: *The breakfast-room of Mrs Swayne's Surrey home. Long oak table centre, laid for breakfast; lavish show of silver and glass. Sideboard, left, laden.*

A thunderstorm rages throughout this play, the thunder conveniently punctuating the dialogue.

Mrs Swayne is seated at table as the curtain rises. Enter LADY FOOTLE.

MRS S: *Dear* Lady Footle! I hope the storm didn't keep you awake?

LADY F: Oh, but it's been fun, watching the lightning strike the houses!

MRS S: Ah, how like you, to look on the bright side!

LADY F: My dear, I make a point of *never* allowing the suffering of others to distress me. Who lived in the quaint old lodge by the gates?

MRS S: Gargoyle, our undergardener. He still does.

LADY F: *Not* any more, dear.

MRS S: Struck?

LADY F: *Mere* rubble. You didn't know?

MRS S: I leave all matters of the estate to my husband. Poor Gargoyle! *Do* take some kidneys.

LADY F: Delicious. (*Heaping plate.*)

MRS S: I'll ring for more toast. (*Pulls bell-rope.*)

CHARLES *shoves open window from outside and pokes his head in. He is wearing a blazer, white flannels, and is carrying a tennis racket. The rain pours down on him in torrents.*

CHARLES: Anyone for tennis?

MRS S: Don't be silly, Charles. Shut the window.

CHARLES: Actually I was wondering if Betty – I mean Miss Swayne —

MRS S: *Shut* the *window*, Charles.

CHARLES: Oh, er, I, er, yes, of course.

Shuts window but remains looking hungrily in, amid lightning.

LADY F (*vaguely*): Charming boy!

MRS S: Yes, but hopelessly unadaptable.

Enter RUBBISH.

Ah, Rubbish! Toast for Lady Footle.

RUBBISH: Yes, madam. (*He removes one or two empty plates, etc.*)

LADY F: A bad storm, Rubbish!

RUBBISH: Yes, my lady.

LADY F: *Splenetic* lightning!

RUBBISH: Quite so, my lady.

LADY F: *Fulminating* thunder!

RUBBISH: Yes, my lady. Intermingled with gunfire.

LADY F: Gunfire?

RUBBISH: Yes, my lady. According to an intelligence from 2LO this morning, this country is in a state of civil war.

MRS S: Civil war?

RUBBISH: Yes, madam. It seems that the Lower Classes, disgruntled with their lot, are rising against their oppressors. More toast, madam?

MRS S: At once, Rubbish. (*Exit* RUBBISH.) Really, I'm sorry that we bought Rubbish that crystal-set. It is putting wild ideas in his head.

Enter BETTY.

Good morning, darling!

BETTY: Mummy darling! (*They rush at each other and embrace.*)

BETTY (*in a 'little girl' voice*): Where's Daddykins?

MRS S: He's at the officekins.

BETTY: Poor Daddykins! (*Sees Charles, and speaks in her normal voice, which is hearty and hockey-playing.*) Oh, look, there's Charles! Isn't he an oaf! (*Lifting cover on sideboard*) Kidneys! Scrumptious!

MRS S: *Where* is Rubbish? *Surely* one can have *toast* when one wishes?

Exit MRS SWAYNE.

BETTY: Lady Footle – aren't you feeling well?

LADY F (*wanly*): Not very, my dear. I am always upset when anyone mentions those *dreadful* poor. Excuse me – I'll go to my room.

Exit LADY FOOTLE.

CHARLES (*bursting open window*): I say – Betty – could you —?

BETTY: I haven't had brekker, Charles.

CHARLES: No, but, Betty, come here a minute.

BETTY (*going over to window, wonderingly*): What is it?

CHARLES: Well, Betty . . . I mean, look here. I mean to say, what?

BETTY: Cough it up, old fruit.

CHARLES: Well, Betty, you must know how I feel about you —

BETTY: Don't rot, Charles.

CHARLES: But I *love* you, dash it. Oh, Lord!

BETTY (*calmly*): Charles, you're rotting, and I haven't had brekker.

Slams window, sending him staggering back. Phone rings.

BETTY (*lifting phone*): Uppercrust 1234?

An oblong of light, like a window, appears in the top right-hand corner of the back wall, revealing Mr Swayne, Betty's Daddy, at the phone. He is keeping a stiff upper lip. He speaks in a clipped, heroic voice.

DADDY: Ah, Betty, listen, darling. I'm afraid I'm in a spot of bother. Don't ask me to explain: there's no time. I just want you to be very very brave. Do you understand?

BETTY (*sweetly calm and serious*): Yes, Daddy.

DADDY: It's the Reds, darling. Taken over. Swarming in the street outside. Hanging all the stockbrokers from lamp-posts. The going's pretty tough.

BETTY: I see.

DADDY: I may not be home for a while. Betty – keep this from your mother.

BETTY: Yes, Daddy.

DADDY (*as a rifle is thrust against the back of his head*): I'm afraid this is it, Betty. Goodbye, darling.

BETTY: Goodbye, Daddy. (*A shot.*) Daddy? (*as* DADDY *falls forward, the oblong of light goes out*) Daddy! (*clicks phone wildly, then becomes icy calm: in a whisper*) Oh, Daddy!

CHARLES *pushes open window and looks in.*

CHARLES: I say, anything wrong?

BETTY (*in a numb voice*): Some beastly Reds have just shot Daddy.

CHARLES: Oh, rotten luck, old girl.

BETTY (*same voice*): It *is* rather hard cheese.

He climbs in. She stretches out a hand, blindly. He takes it in both his own.

CHARLES: I say, Betty, I'll . . . stand by you, and all that.

BETTY (*huskily*): You're jolly decent, Charles.

Enter MRS SWAYNE.

MRS S: Rubbish has *disappeared*! Charles, stop dripping rain on the carpet and go home. Who was on the phone, dear?

BETTY: Mummy, it was Daddy. He told me . . . he might be home . . . late.

MRS S (*briskly*): Well, no need to dramatize it, dear.

BETTY: No . . . of course not, Mummy.

CHARLES (*eagerly*): Actually, Mrs Swayne, Betty is being jolly brave and hiding it from you that Mr Swayne has been killed by a lot of rotten Reds —

BETTY *hits him in the stomach with her elbow.*

CHARLES (*with a gasp*): I say! What? Oh, I mean to say: yes, of course.

MRS S: Killed by Reds? What nonsense!

BETTY: Yes, of course. Nonsense.

CHARLES: Yes, rather!

MRS S: You're mad!

CHARLES: Oh, I say! I mean yes, I suppose so!

MRS S: Go home!

CHARLES: Oh, but – oh, all right.

Exit through window into rain.

MRS S: I can't imagine what's happened to Rubbish. Without him, we can't have any toast.

BETTY: I don't want any brekker, actually.

MRS S: Don't be absurd: of course you do.

Pulls bell-rope several times, angrily.
Really, this is most irregular!
BETTY: Perhaps we'd better look for him.
MRS S: But it's so difficult, dear. I mean, he'll be in the *kitchen*.
BETTY: Yes, it *is* jolly awkward. Couldn't we sort of – scout around in a general sort of way?
MRS S: Oh, well, I suppose we must. But it's most irregular.
Exit, followed by Betty, right.
Enter RUBBISH, *left, followed by two* REDS, *holding shotguns.*
FIRST RED: What effete room is this?
RUBBISH: This is the breakfast-room, sir.
SECOND RED (*punching him in the stomach and chopping him heavily in the neck as he doubles up*): Don't call him *sir*. It's the jargon of the lackey class.
RUBBISH: No, sir.
SECOND RED (*thumping him again*): Comrade!
RUBBISH: Comrade, sir.
SECOND RED (*thumping him again*): Just *comrade*, comrade. Comrade, for equality and freedom!
FIRST RED: So! This is the breakfast-room, is it? (*Wanders round, discovers covered dishes on sideboard.*) Ha! Bourgeois food! (*Removes cover.*) Parts of dead bodies! Disgusting!
SECOND RED (*to Rubbish*): Our comrade is vegetarian. He abhors cruelty of any kind.
FIRST RED (*looking through window*): We could erect the guillotine in the garden.
SECOND RED: Ah – on the terrace! Excellent! Then this room could be our court-room.
RUBBISH: C-c-court-room?
SECOND RED: Certainly. Every capitalist must be tried before execution. To do otherwise would be antisocial.
FIRST RED: Let me explain, comrade. You have the immense good fortune to live in the house which the Grand Committee has chosen, for strategical reasons, as its headquarters in Surrey. Here will the tumbrils come; here the heads will roll; here the flag of freedom, Southern area, sub-section F, will fly. Is it not glorious?

RUBBISH: H-h-heads? R-r-roll?

FIRST RED (*kindly*): Have no fear, comrade. We probably shall not execute you.

SECOND RED: No. We do not blame you for being what you are. You are merely the degenerate end-product of an obsolescent society.

FIRST RED: You are probably capable of redemption, with training.

SECOND RED: Fifteen years in a correction-centre, and another five shovelling dung in one of our glorious collective farms!

FIRST RED: By which time, who knows, you may be reintegrated!

SECOND RED: Is it not glorious? But – (*Moving to phone*) we must ring Grand H.Q.

FIRST RED: Wait, comrade. We should inspect the house first. Who knows what they may be hiding? (*To Rubbish, prodding him with rifle.*) Conduct me, comrade! You, comrade (*To second Red*) will remain here, on guard against counter-revolutionary reprisals.

Exeunt FIRST RED *and* RUBBISH. *Re-enter* MRS SWAYNE *and* BETTY, *left.*

SECOND RED (*swinging round and levelling shotgun*): Ha!

MRS S (*undaunted*): Oh, a visitor! How rude you must think us, letting you wander in unannounced like this! I *do* apologize!

SECOND RED (*taken aback, thickly*): Now—

MRS S (*continuing with hardly a pause*): The fact is, we've (*Confidentially roguish*) *mislaid our butler!* (*Tinkling laugh.*) Isn't it ridiculous? Let me take your things!

He stands amazed as she plucks his shotgun from his hand. After a distinct pause she removes his felt hat from his head. He is bald, and passes an embarrassed hand over his pate. MRS SWAYNE *makes for exit, right.*

SECOND RED (*his self-possession gone*): — I want that back. (*Indicates shotgun.*)

MRS S (*turning at door, with dignity*): Well: of course! I shall put it in the umbrella stand. (*Exit.*)

BETTY (*chummy and hearty*): Look here, *do* sit down, won't you?

(*With inspiration.*) You wouldn't care for some breakfast, would you? I mean, there's *oodles* of kidneys here – and some bacon – also some passable coffee —

SECOND RED (*wavering, as she holds the dishes before him*): Well – I . . . oh, all right. It'll leave less for the bourgeoisie.

BETTY (*heaping his plate*): I don't quite get that. I'm afraid I'm not awfully brainy. (*Going towards exit, right*) I'll get you some toast.

SECOND RED (*harshly*): Stay where you are!

BETTY: Now, don't you be stuffy, like Mummy! (*Twiddles her fingers at him.*) Back soon! (*Exit.*)

The window bursts open and CHARLES *climbs in, panting.*

CHARLES (*seeing second Red*): Oh! I say, excuse me butting in like this, but I've just dashed back to warn the family, what?

SECOND RED: Warn them?

CHARLES: Yes, rather. All the roads are blocked. Revolution! Incredible, what?

SECOND RED: Ha! (*He continues eating.*)

CHARLES: I admire your calm, old boy. (*Enter* BETTY *with a plate of toast.*) I say, Betty, the dashed Reds are everywhere. It's a bally siege!

BETTY: Go on? (*To second Red*) Well, I'm awfully glad you're here. It's nice to have a shooting man about the house.

SECOND RED: So! You want me to shoot Reds for you?

BETTY: Yes, if any come.

SECOND RED: Ha! Well, I'd better have my gun back, hadn't I?

BETTY: Oh, gosh, yes, of course! (*Exit.*)

CHARLES: Marksman, eh? Jolly good. Backs to the wall, what?

SECOND RED: You never said a truer word.

Re-enter BETTY, *with shotgun.*

Ha! (*Takes it from her.*) Now: go over to the window, both of you, and put up your hands!

CHARLES: I say, don't rot, old boy. The dashed Empire's at stake!

BETTY (*quietly*): Do as he says, Charles. (*She goes to the window.*)

CHARLES: But do you mean to say he's —

BETTY: I'm afraid so.

CHARLES: Well, I'm dashed. I shall jolly well write to *The Times*! (*Joins her.*)

SECOND RED: Silence!

CHARLES (*indignantly*): You needn't think I'm going to hobnob with you, you working-class bounder!

Enter RUBBISH, MRS SWAYNE, LADY FOOTLE, *with their hands up, followed by the* FIRST RED, *with shotgun.*

FIRST RED: Ah! Good work, comrade. (*To his captives*) Join them by the window!

They do so.

SECOND RED: Have you scoured the house?

FIRST RED: Yes, and (*Indicating his captives*) removed this scum!

CHARLES: There are ladies present, you know!

FIRST RED: 'Lady' will be an obsolete word very soon. There will be nothing but comrades.

MRS S: And how will you achieve this chummy state of affairs?

FIRST RED: By liquidating our enemies!

BETTY: So there'll be nothing left but friends!

FIRST RED: Exactly!

CHARLES: Well, I must say that's jolly neat!

FIRST RED: Oh, yes indeed. Dialectically so. But mark you, we shall not kill everybody.

LADY F: How forbearing of you!

FIRST RED: Some shall be spared for the farms, others for the mines. (*Pointing to Charles*) You, for example – you might do well for the mines.

CHARLES: You mean *coal* mines?

FIRST RED: Of course.

CHARLES: But what about tennis, dash it?

FIRST RED: Ah, the new society will have no room for boss-class games. Men will use their muscles for the State. Production will be our watchword.

SECOND RED: Under our glorious Five Year Plan, with amendment B!

FIRST RED (*quickly*): Ah, no, comrade. Excuse me. A slip of the tongue, no doubt. You mean to say, amendment *D*.

SECOND RED: But excuse me. Amendment *B*, which is in strict accordance with our ideology.

FIRST RED: Oh no, I insist: amendment D. Amendment B has been proved spurious, erroneous, and reactionary.

SECOND RED (*angrily*): Come: amendment D is deviationist, re-visionist, and counter-revolutionary!

They glare at each other in rage and consternation.

FIRST RED (*panting slightly*): D!

SECOND RED (*hissing*): B!

LADY F (*with resignation*): Can't you two agree? My arms are nearly dropping off.

SECOND RED: There can be no agreeing with a traitor.

BETTY: No need to take it *seriously*, surely?

MRS S: It's only a technicality, isn't it? Or have you liquidated those too?

CHARLES: You fellers have got to pull together, what? Team spirit, and all that!

FIRST RED: I will not compromise with a reactionary.

MRS S: Nonsense. You'll have to, if you want your ridiculous New World.

LADY F: One must learn to give and take in this life, mustn't one?

SECOND RED: I'll not give anything to a Fascist pig!

FIRST RED: What should I take from a Trotskyist hyena?

Their voices rise hysterically.

MRS S: Come: you are both saying things you will regret.

LADY F: You are even in danger of losing your self-control.

FIRST RED (*weeping, sobbing, dancing about and waving his fists*): Bah! Bourgeois scum! What do *you* know about it? (*To second Red*) As for you – *comrade* – ha ha! – counter revolutionary crypto-Trotskyist deviationist!

SECOND RED: Obsolescent neo-Fascist reactionary!

FIRST RED: Ideology-ignoring pseudo-bourgeois opportunist!

SECOND RED: Dialectic-logged anti-proletarian empiricist!

They both gasp for breath.

FIRST RED (*searching frantically for words of abuse*): Drip!

SECOND RED (*in a similar state*): Weed!

For a few moments they confront each other, trembling and panting. Then they both raise their shotguns, fire, and fall simultaneously.

MRS S: Well, really!

CHARLES: By Jove!

LADY F: *Utter* lack of self-control!

BETTY: What about the Revolution?

MRS S: What about my carpet? Rubbish, please see to the disposal of (*Pointing to corpses*) – these.

RUBBISH: Yes, madam. Meanwhile I will arrange the bodies in seemly attitudes.

MRS S: Yes; and *cover* them with something, please.

Phone rings.

BETTY: I'll answer it. Hallo?

The oblong lights up as before. It is Betty's Daddy.

DADDY: Hallo, Betty darling.

BETTY: Daddy!! So you're not dead, after all!

DADDY: No, no. Bullet grazed my temple. Rotten shot. A bit dazed, that's all.

BETTY: But this Revolution —

DADDY: It's over.

BETTY: Over?

DADDY: Yes. The Reds have had some sort of quarrel among themselves. Can't make head or tail of it. Something about —

BETTY: Amendment B or Amendment D!

DADDY: So you've heard? Good Lord. Anyway, not one of them's left alive. All shot one another. Extraordinary fellows.

BETTY: Well, but that's good, isn't it!

DADDY: Well, yes, in a way. It'll send up the taxes, though. No working classes left, you see. Someone's got to pay. We know who! Well: tell Mummy I'll be home on time, after all. Goodbye, darling.

BETTY: Goodbye, Daddy. (*Replaces phone.*) That was Daddy! He isn't dead!

MRS S: Don't be silly, dear, of course he's not! I gather that this absurd Revolution is over? (BETTY *nods.*) Good! Then we can all get back to normal, like decent people. Charles, go home!

CHARLES: Well, actually —

LADY F (*looking at him keenly*): Do you know, the rain has stopped! Dear Mrs Swayne, please show me round your garden.

MRS S: But — (LADY F *nudges her and gesticulates theatrically towards Charles and Betty*.) Oh. But good Heavens, the boy's an idiot. Oh, very well. Come, then.

LADY F: I am sure to be *nonplussed* by the hollyhocks!

Exeunt MRS S, LADY F, *and* RUBBISH.

BETTY (*looking down at the corpses*): Why did they say *ha*! and *comrade,* and use those queer long words?

CHARLES: Queer chaps altogether. Communists, y'know.

BETTY: You are clever, Charles, understanding these things.

CHARLES: Do you like me, Betty?

BETTY: Of course, Charles. You're a jolly decent chap.

CHARLES: Betty — Look here, I'm sick of staring in at you through the window, dash it! Will you – (*Gulps*) – marry me?

BETTY (*amazed*): Marry you?

CHARLES: Yes, rather!

BETTY: But what for?

CHARLES: Eh? Well, then we could share the same tennis court, what?

BETTY (*doubtfully*): Ye-es, but . . . You wouldn't keep rotting about . . . *love* and all that, would you?

CHARLES: Oh, I say. Well, no. All the same, *that* does come into it, doesn't it? I was thinking we might have a —

BETTY: Charles, please! (*Turns away, embarrassed, and walks up left.*)

CHARLES (*following*): I was going to say, a dog!

BETTY (*in an altered tone*): A dog!

CHARLES: Yes, rather!

BETTY (*all her amorous and maternal instincts aroused*): Oh, that's a ripping idea! I love doggies!

CHARLES: Well, there you are then, what? How about it?

BETTY: Well, all right!

CHARLES: Jolly good!

Enter RUBBISH, *with a sheet.*

Ah, Rubbish!

RUBBISH (*covering bodies with sheet*): Yes, sir. More toast, sir?

CHARLES: By Jove, this family has a mania for toast! No, no, Rubbish: not *more* toast; *a* toast!

He seizes a decanter from the sideboard, pours three drinks, and thrusts one upon Rubbish.

RUBBISH: What is the toast, sir?

BETTY: *You* propose it, Rubbish!

RUBBISH: Thank you, Miss Betty. Very well. (*Raises glass.*) To the Solidarity of the Middle Classes!

They stare at him, blankly.

To the Solidarity of the Middle Classes! Er – your glass, sir? – Miss?

BETTY
CHARLES } (*uncomprehendingly*): To the Solidarity of the Middle Classes!

RUBBISH: Quite so. Excuse me, sir: Miss. (*Exit.*)

BETTY (*puzzled*): Funny old Rubbish!

CHARLES: What did he mean, do you think?

BETTY: Haven't the faintest! (*She pauses for a couple of moments.*) I'm afraid I'm not very brainy. . . .

CURTAIN

Is Horror Your Neighbour?

A Tussaud Horror

CHARACTERS

GUIDE
VISITOR
SYKES THE STRANGLER
BROWN THE BODYSNATCHER
JANE THE RIPPER
PINK THE POISONER
BLACK THE MULTIPLE MURDERER
HANGMAN
HANGED
EXECUTIONER
EXECUTED

IS HORROR YOUR NEIGHBOUR?

SCENE: *The Chamber of Horrors at Madame Tussaud's.*

ENTER *the* GUIDE, *left, before the closed curtain. He speaks over his shoulder as he moves, halting at the partition of the curtains.*

GUIDE: Well, sir, this is the Chamber of Horrors. Do you still want to go through with it?

Enter VISITOR.

VISITOR: Oh, yes, I think so. Well, I mean, I'm sure I do. You're offering a hundred pounds to anyone who'll spend the night in this place, and I could do with a hundred pounds.

GUIDE: Not much use to you when you're stark stiff with terror, sir. Very few of 'em come out sane in the morning. Take my advice, sir – turn back!

VISITOR: No, no. I've got a-nerves of steel. Go ahead.

GUIDE: All right. In we go.

He makes as though to turn a key, and the curtains part.

Dim lighting reveals nine models grouped around the stage. Sykes, Brown, Pink, and Black are on pedestals in the foreground, with Jane the Ripper seated, centre, an open razor held elegantly above her head. To the rear of these models are the Hangman and the Hanged man, and the Executioner and his victim.

GUIDE: There you are, sir. Pretty little lot, aren't they?

VISITOR (*A trifle shaken*): Look kind of . . . *real,* don't they?

GUIDE: Ah, it's a good job they're not sir! This one (*Pointing to Sykes*) was Sykes, the Strangler. He had six wives. They never discovered their bodies.

VISITOR: I bet those wives could tell some tales!

GUIDE: Yes, sir. Old wives tales. Now this (*Indicating Brown*) was Brown, the Bodysnatcher. Look at his eyes! Evil aren't they?

VISITOR (*pathetically facetious, addressing Brown as he passes him*): Good evening!

GUIDE: And now, here we have ...

BROWN (*from the side of his mouth*): 'Evening.

VISITOR (*spinning round in alarm*): Hey! I say – did you hear that?

GUIDE: Hear what, sir?

VISITOR: He – he said good evening to me!

GUIDE: Impossible, sir. Your nerves are playing you tricks.

VISITOR: I – I suppose so.

GUIDE: Well, as I was saying. This is Pink, the Poisoner, and this is the Multiple Murderer, Black, who boiled his victims alive, and disposed of their bodies by eating them.

VISITOR (*horrified*): Wh – what, while they were still alive?

GUIDE: Wouldn't put anything past him, sir. (*He turns back to Jane.*) And now, sir, finally like, last but not least, your favourite and mine, the Female Fiend of Dusseldorf – Jane the Ripper!

VISITOR: Good Heavens! What a hag!

GUIDE (*gloomily humorous*): Careful, sir. She may be listening. Well, I must leave you now. Good night, sir, and – good luck.
Exit GUIDE.

THE VISITOR, *after an apprehensive glance at the Models, comes down centre and sits gingerly on a chair, his back to them.*

The lights change to green, and as they change, a slow movement from the models is perceptible. Then SYKES THE STRANGLER *steps deliberately down from his pedestal, and points a slow finger at the Visitor.*

SYKES: Now, with hope locked out, and him locked in,

MODELS (*together*): Let the midnight orgy of human demons begin. (BROWN THE BODYSNATCHER *steps down.*)

BROWN: Fool, to share a chamber with such as we,

MODELS (*together*): Whose bones make ghastly music on the gallows-tree! (PINK THE POISONER *steps down.*)

PINK: Fear shall fret his heart till sanity break.

MODELS: This is a dream from which he shall never awake!
(BLACK THE MULTIPLE MURDERER *steps down.*)

BLACK: Tremble, boy, for evil is our endless labour: (JANE THE RIPPER *rises and stands forward.*)

JANE: What foul form stands at your side?

MODELS: IS HORROR YOUR NEIGHBOUR?

The VISITOR, *who has been showing signs of increasing uneasiness throughout this chant, suddenly springs up, his back still to the models. They step silently back to their positions and freeze. With desperate courage the* VISITOR *swings round to face them. They are, of course, exactly as they were when he came in.*

VISITOR (*in a high-pitched voice*): They *moved*! I know they did! They're creeping up on me while my back's turned. (*He looks wildly about, and espies a bucket, left, which he picks up and places at the foot of Sykes.*) There! Now, if he moves, he'll kick the bucket! N-not a bad joke, that, in the circumstances.

SYKES *stoops quickly, picks up the bucket, and hangs it on the arm of Brown. The* VISITOR *turns, sees that it has been moved, and gives a cry of horror.*

VISITOR: No, no! It can't be! I'm seeing things! My nerves are playing me tricks! I know what I'll do! I'll whistle to keep my spirits up!

VISITOR: (*whistling the tune*): There's an old mill by the stream —

MODELS (*together, with terrific gusto*): NELLIE DEAN!

Visitor is panic-stricken. The MODELS *point their fingers at him, screaming with savagely derisive laughter. He runs up and down, all control shattered.*

VISITOR (*yelling above the din*): Help! Help! Help! Help!

The MODELS *are suddenly still and silent, but the* VISITOR *continues shrieking.*

VISITOR: Help, help, HELP!

Enter GUIDE.

GUIDE (*as before, gloomily calm*): Anything wrong, sir?

VISITOR: Gi – give me something for my nerves, quick!

A great change comes over the Guide. His manner is charged with overwhelming brightness.

GUIDE: Something for your *Nerves*, sir? Oh, yes!, sir I know the VERY THING!

He runs out, to return immediately with a huge bottle.

GUIDE: NERVO for the nerves, sir!

The Chamber is flooded with light.

MODELS (*together, with immense enthusiasm*): Ah: NERVO!

JANE THE RIPPER rises and minces right up to the footlights.

JANE (*to the audience, in a most ingratiating voice*): Are you run-down, nervous, a prey to unnecessary fears? Can't sleep? No appetite? Then take NERVO, the finest of all Nerve Tonics. Obtainable from all chemists, prices one-and-nine and three shillings; and remember – the larger bottle contains three times as much as the smaller.

SYKES, BROWN, PINK and BLACK step from their pedestals and stand four abreast. The HANGMAN, the EXECUTIONER, and their victims watch them with radiant approval.

SYKES: When you're in a fearful fright,

MODELS (*together*): NERVO soon will put you right!

BLACK: NERVO for the highly-strung,

MODELS (*together*): NERVO for the old and young!

VISITOR (*beaming*): I'll *certainly* buy a bottle of NERVO *right away*!

JANE THE RIPPER and the GUIDE bow to the audience, and as they straighten up, pick up from the floor a large placard which bears the inscription – ADVT.

CURTAIN

A Villa On Venus

A Cosmic Absurdity

CHARACTERS

SHAM ⎫
GIMBLE ⎭ *citizens of the Planet Venus*

FRANK FEARLESS ⎫
DICK DREADNOUGHT ⎬ *visitors from the Planet Earth*
BILL BOLD ⎭

SIX BUG-EYED MONSTERS

SPIV, *a salesman from the Planet Mercury*

A VILLA ON VENUS

SCENE: *A Landscape in Northern Venus.*
TIME: *The Present Day.*

The curtain rises on a scene which, though distinctly unworldly, is not unfamiliar to us, for we have seen similar scenes often enough on the covers of Science-Fiction Magazines. The background is a conglomeration of futuristic machinery and exotic vegetation. Down left is an equally futuristic seat, and up right, a Reflector, which resembles a large shaving-mirror mounted on a revolving stand. Into this, SHAM *is gazing intently.*

SHAM: Gimble!

GIMBLE (*off-stage, left*): Yes, guv?

SHAM: Come here a minute, will you?

GIMBLE (*off-stage*): All right, I'm coming.

Enter GIMBLE. *He and Sham, whose flesh is a bright golden colour, are both dressed in simple Grecian tunics. Sham, much the older of the two, is a genial little creature, cultured in voice, kindly and worldly-wise in manner. Gimble is young, brisk, and efficient; and he speaks, curiously enough, in a strong Cockney accent.*

GIMBLE: What is it? Someone landing?

SHAM: Yes, and I don't like the look of it. Take a look in the reflector, Gimble, will you? Your eyes are better than mine.
He crosses to the seat, left.

GIMBLE (*manipulating Reflector*): Can't see a thing . . . Ah, wait a bit, though. Yes I can.

SHAM: Where are they from, that's the point?

GIMBLE: Hard to say. Not Jupiter.

SHAM: No.

GIMBLE: Not Mars, either.

SHAM: No.

GIMBLE: Well, really, I've never seen a crate like this before. Looks as if its come out of the Ark. In fact, I'm not sure it *isn't* the Ark . . . Do you know, it may sound crazy, but —

SHAM: Well?

GIMBLE: I think they're from the Earth!

SHAM (*grimly*): Exactly! The Red Planet.

GIMBLE: Oh, but they couldn't be. They're living in the Dark Ages down there!

SHAM: That's no argument. It'd be just like them to invent some fantastic craft centuries after all the other planets have done it, and then think themselves lords of the Universe. What do you bet me they start offering us coloured beads when they get here?

GIMBLE: They might not get here! You should see this thing rocking about!

SHAM: Well, I wish them no harm, but I don't like this. I've watched the Earth through the instruments for years, and I wouldn't exactly call the natives friendly.

GIMBLE: Act rather queer, don't they?

SHAM: They're raving mad, my son. They keep blowing one another to bits.

GIMBLE: Oh, well, that's all right then. They'll blow one another to bits, and we'll go on living our dignified lives.

SHAM: No, you don't quite understand. What I mean is —

GIMBLE (*with a shout*): They're through! They're going to land! . . . Easy, now, Earthmen. Gently does it . . . Nose her down . . . Steady, steady . . . Blimey! They're going to crash!

He dives off, left, in alarm, with SHAM *after him. From off-stage right there is an ear-splitting crash, several rolling echoes, and a series of flashes. The faces of Sham and Gimble appear cautiously from the Wings.*

GIMBLE: What a rotten landing!

SHAM: Sh! Here they come.

They withdraw their heads. Enter FRANK FEARLESS, DICK DREADNOUGHT, *and* BILL BOLD, *tugging off their space-helmets. Their dress is as familiar as the scenery: for they are wearing the space-suits we have seen so often in magazines and on the screen. They place their helmets on the ground, well to the rear, stretch, and inhale deeply.*

FRANK: Thank goodness to get that thing off! Some fool cleaned the inside with paraffin!

DICK: Awfully hot, isn't it?

BILL (*waving an arm at the scenery*): We're in the South, I imagine.

SHAM (*off-stage*): Lucky for you you're not!

FRANK: Strange! I thought I heard a voice!

DICK: So did I.

BILL: An echo, no doubt.

DICK: Now that's just silly. You said, 'We're in the South, I imagine.' How could that echo back as 'Lucky for you you're not'?

GIMBLE (*off-stage*): Shows he's thinking, anyway.

FRANK (*casting an eye over the immensely complicated machinery in the background*): It's possible, I suppose, that there may be *life* here, in a primitive form.

SHAM (*off-stage*): Thank you, sir.

DICK: There it is again – that sound!

BILL (*resolutely*): I'm going to investigate this!

SHAM (*emerging, followed by Gimble*): Don't bother. Good evening, gentlemen.

FRANK: Good Lord! Things from Another World!

GIMBLE (*irritated*): Cheek! Who got here first?

DICK: It speaks English!

BILL (*roaring with laughter*): Ha ha ha! Look at its face!

FRANK: Steady, fellows. I shall try to speak to it. Er – greetings, creatures.

SHAM: Greetings to you. Have a toffee.

DICK: Steady, Frank. May be poisoned.

FRANK: No, no. We must humour them. Er – how does one eat this sort of thing?

GIMBLE: Well, one puts it in one's mouth, one moves one's jaws about, and finally one swallows.

FRANK (*with dignity*): I see. And now – how is it that you are speaking English?

SHAM (*to Gimble, with a gesture of resignation*): Oh, it's like talking to a savage! (*To Frank*) Well, you see, the air here is charged with rays which turn our thoughts into a common language. To you, I seem to be speaking English – to me, you seem to be speaking *my* language.

FRANK: Ah, I see. We have something of the sort on the Earth.

DICK: It's called United Nations.

BILL: Only it doesn't work.

SHAM: If it isn't a personal question, why have you come to Venus?

FRANK: Ah, Venus has always lured Man.

DICK: We are here in the name of Progress.

SHAM: Oh. We're here in the name of (*introducing Gimble*) Gimble, and (*bowing*) Sham. (*He points to the ray-guns which the Earthmen are holding.*) And what are those?

BILL (*flourishing gun*): These are ray-guns. They can blow an elephant to bits at a distance of two miles.

GIMBLE: And you've got those in the name of Progress too, I suppose?

FRANK: Yes, of course. The natives must be shown who is their master. But don't worry – you seem friendly little beings. We shan't shoot you.

GIMBLE: That's very kind of you.

FRANK: We are driven by an insatiable craving for Progress. All our race have this urge. We are the first Men on Venus, but soon, others will come, spurred by our example —

SHAM: How delightful!

FRANK: They will overrun the Solar System. They will embrace the great nebulae. They will take the sun.

GIMBLE: Well, be careful where you take it, mate. It's useful.

DICK (*eagerly*): Frank's right. Before long, every housewife on the Earth will own a villa on Venus.

GIMBLE: And what about us?

BILL: Ah, to you will fall the honour of being Man's first interplanetary assistant.

SHAM: Well, well, well . . . Anyway, it's a good job you didn't land in the South.

DICK: So you said before. Why?

SHAM: The B.E.M.s live in the South.

FRANK: B.E.M.s?

GIMBLE: The B.E.M.s – the Bug-Eyed Monsters.

FRANK: Come, come! Bug-Eyed Monsters exist only in the cheapest fiction.

SHAM: I'm afraid life's rather like the cheapest fiction, my boy.

BILL: But what are they like – the B.E.M.s?

GIMBLE: Cor – like nothing on Earth.

SHAM: But don't worry. They never come here.

DICK: Now that's a pity. These creatures must be most interesting phenomena. We might have got some pictures of them.

GIMBLE (*furiously*): Look, mate, the B.E.M.s are not going to pose for you while you tell 'em to watch the birdy! They're really nasty, those things are, and we don't want 'em here, see?

FRANK: Well, they don't come here anyway, according to you.

GIMBLE: You never know. *They* might want to take pictures of *you*.

SHAM: Come, this is getting us nowhere. I think that before you gentlemen make any more – er – progress, you'd better have some supper.

GIMBLE: It won't be poison. We don't eat poison.

SHAM: Come, Gimble. Sit down, gentlemen. We'll call you when supper's ready.

Exit SHAM *and* GIMBLE. *The* EARTHMEN *sit on the seat, left.*

FRANK: Quaint little creatures, aren't they? Almost human.

DICK: Very simple-minded, though.

BILL: Oh, rather. What stuff about Bug-Eyed Monsters!

Enter, left, a BUG-EYED MONSTER. *It wears a long green cloak, black tights, and a green hood, from which stares a green and demoniac face. Grinning wickedly, it lurks behind the Earthmen, listening as they chat.*

DICK: Pure children's-comic stuff!

FRANK: Oh, I entirely agree. I for one don't believe in B.E.M.s for a moment.

The B.E.M. *moves silently to centre, and beckons. Enter five more* B.E.M.S, *exactly like the first, from right. They form a line, centre to right. The First* B.E.M. *stands downstage, a little apart from the others.*

DICK: I intend to write an article about the childish beliefs of the beings on Venus.

BILL: I wonder if this supper's ready? I expect — (*In consternation.*) Hey! Look, chaps – look!

The EARTHMEN *spring to their feet, see the B.E.M.s and back away apprehensively.*

FIRST B.E.M.: Greetings, Earthmen!

FRANK (*gulping*): Er – yes, of course. Greetings.

FIRST B.E.M.: We observed your arrival, and hurried here to greet you.

DICK: V-very good of you.

FIRST B.E.M.: Good? Please don't use that unpleasant language here. We despise goodness.

BILL: But what do you want to do?

B.E.M.s (*exultantly*): WE WORK FOR THE DESTRUCTION OF MANKIND.

SECOND B.E.M. (*stepping forward*): Yes. For many years we have had visitors to Venus from other planets – Mercury, Mars, Jupiter, Saturn. But they have all been creatures of peace, and have used their science to keep us away. Always have we turned our longing eyes on your planet, for you and we – ah! we can work together so beautifully for the death of man!

B.E.M.s (*joyfully*): DEATH! THE DEATH OF MAN!

THIRD B.E.M. (*stepping forward*): For your planet, the red planet Earth, is the planet of Murder and Death.

B.E.M.s: MURDER AND DEATH!

FOURTH B.E.M. (*stepping forward*): Join us, Earthmen, in our great plan to destroy Mankind!

FIFTH B.E.M. (*stepping forward*): Help us to launch the avalanche of our rage!

SIXTH B.E.M. (*stepping forward*): Hasten with us to the Day of Doom!

B.E.M.s: DOOM!

But the Earthmen are extremely indignant.

FRANK: Now look here, you rotten blighters – you've got us all wrong!

BILL: We wouldn't dream of joining your disgusting plot.

DICK: You can jolly well put your hands up, and don't try any tricks, because these guns can blow an elephant to bits at two miles!

FIRST B.E.M.: Ha ha! (*To the others*) *Hypnotize* these men!
The B.E.M.S *swing their arms rhythmically, crooning as they do so –*
Whoo . . . Whoo . . . Bonk!
– and at the 'bonk!' the Earthmen are struck rigid.

FIRST B.E.M.: Excellent! Now, in their trance, they will tell us all the secrets of their life on Earth! Right, men – On to Doom!

B.E.M.S: ON TO DOOM!
They file out, leaving the Earthmen still transfixed. The last B.E.M. *puts his head round the curtain.*

B.E.M.: Er – follow us, please.
Arms outstretched like sleepwalkers, the EARTHMEN *follow.*
Re-enter SHAM *and* GIMBLE, *who carries a tray with three covered dishes on it.*

SHAM: Well, here you are, gents . . . Well! where have they got to?

GIMBLE: Gone exploring, maybe. (*He sets down the tray.*)

SHAM: After all our trouble, too. What bad manners.

GIMBLE (*sniffing the air*): Just a minute. Can you smell something?

SHAM (*sniffing*): Yes, now that you mention it.

GIMBLE: Rather like sulphur, isn't it?

SHAM: Yes, it is, rather —
They stare at each other, suddenly.

SHAM
GIMBLE } (*together*): *Sulphur!*

SHAM (*greatly alarmed*): The B.E.M.s have got them!

GIMBLE: Talk about birds of a feather!

SHAM (*sitting down*): I suppose we ought to rescue them.

GIMBLE (*joining him on the seat*): Yes . . . We'll start tomorrow, shall we?

SHAM: Hallo! (*pointing into wings, right.*) There's someone coming

GIMBLE: Why, it's that salesman fellow from Mercury. It's old Spiv. Hi-ya, Spiv!

Enter SPIV. *He is dressed like Sham and Gimble, and resemble them, but that he looks old and very weary. He lugs an enormous suit case.*

SHAM (*going forward to shake his hand*): Hallo, Spiv! I haven't seen you for ages!

GIMBLE (*with sympathy*): You look a bit done up, cocker. Come and sit down and rest your feet.

SPIV *sinks down, planting the suitcase at his feet.*

SPIV: That's the way I feel. (*Without hope.*) You don't want to buy a death-ray, do you?

SHAM: No, thank you.

SPIV: It'll wipe out a whole city.

SHAM: Well, when I want to wipe out a whole city, I'll remember you.

SPIV (*dejectedly*): They all talk like that nowadays.

GIMBLE: Business is bad, is it mate?

SPIV: Terrible. I go up and down the Solar System, calling on all the planets until I'm worn out, but no one wants to buy weapons any more. Peace and concord – nothing but peace and concord wherever I go. It's awful.

GIMBLE: Not very nice, though, is it, selling things that kill people?

SPIV: What can I do? It's my bread and butter. I suppose I could get another job, but that's not easy at my time of life.

SHAM: You might sell to the B.E.M.s.

SPIV (*shocked*): Oh, no, no. I've got some conscience left.

SHAM: Well – why don't you try the Earth?

SPIV (*considering*): The planet Earth? . . . No, not worth bothering about. They're too backward. (*He rises wearily.*) The fact is, I'm finished. (*He picks up his case and walks to centre.*) They just don't want machines of death any more. Books of poetry now – they sell like hot cakes.

SHAM: I do wish I could help you, Spiv.

SPIV: I know you would if you could, old chap.

GIMBLE: Perhaps a lovely war will break out somewhere. Keep your chin up.

SPIV: No such luck. But thanks for listening. So long, fellows.

SHAM
GIMBLE } *(together)*: So long, Spiv.

Exit SPIV.

GIMBLE: Poor old Spiv, selling weapons in a peaceful Universe!

SHAM *(gazing after him)*: Yes, it's a shame . . . What! Some more visitors? *(Suddenly)* Gimble! Watch out! It's the B.E.M.s!

SHAM *and* GIMBLE *take up a defensive position behind the seat as the* B.E.M.S *troop in.*

GIMBLE: Now look here – if you want trouble you'll get it. We don't want you nasty things round here!

SHAM: Go away!

FIRST B.E.M. *(anxiously)*: No, listen, Sham —

SHAM: Sham? Who do you think you're talking to? Get out!

FIRST B.E.M.: No, please listen.

SHAM: Oh, all right. What is it?

FIRST B.E.M.: Please help us to get rid of these *ghastly* Earthmen!

SHAM: Why, what's wrong with them?

FIRST B.E.M.: *Wrong* with them? They're *unspeakable*.

GIMBLE: Then why did you kidnap them?

FIRST B.E.M.: Oh, we were in the wrong, we admit it. But we didn't realize that anything could be so vile.

SHAM: I thought that you objects worked 'for the destruction of mankind', or something?

FIRST B.E.M.: Yes, yes, but there's a difference between healthy destruction and the horrors we've been told.

SECOND B.E.M.: We put them in a trance, and they described their life on the Earth.

THIRD B.E.M.: Their squalid days!

FOURTH B.E.M.: Their piggish nights!

FIFTH B.E.M.: Their beastly world of business, and their poisonous ways of pleasure!

SIXTH B.E.M.: Their repulsive insurance companies, banks and offices!

SECOND B.E.M.: Their ratlike houses, hotels and clubs!

THIRD B.E.M.: Their trains and tubes and buses and bicycles!

FOURTH B.E.M.: Their prisons and palaces and aerodromes and asylums!

FIFTH B.E.M.: Their luxury liners!

SIXTH B.E.M.: Their cafés and cinemas!

SECOND B.E.M.: Their picnics on the beach!

THIRD B.E.M.: Their dances on the lawn!

FOURTH B.E.M.: Their food, beds, funerals, baths!

FIFTH B.E.M.: Their men!

SIXTH B.E.M.: Their women!

B.E.M.s (*together*): THEIR BEASTLY LIVES!

FIRST B.E.M.: And after all that, what do you think one of them said? I'll tell you. He said, 'In time, every housewife on the Earth will own a villa on Venus!'

SHAM (*calmly*): Well, you've really let yourselves in for it this time, haven't you?

FIRST B.E.M.: It'll be just as bad for you.

SHAM: Oh no, it won't. They'll all want to live in the South, you'll see.

B.E.M.s *groan*.

FIRST B.E.M. (*deeply dejected*): Ah, well, we don't deserve it, I suppose. All right, men – on to Doom.

B.E.M.s (*croaking dismally*): On to Doom.

They begin to shamble away.

SHAM: Wait! I've changed my mind!

B.E.M.s (*returning jubilantly*): Hooray!

SHAM: Quiet! Gimble, go after Spiv and bring him back, will you?

GIMBLE: Right, guv. (*Exit* GIMBLE.)

FIRST B.E.M.: You're really going to help us?

SHAM: Yes. I never thought I'd have any fellow-feeling for a Bug-Eyed Monster, but circumstances alter cases. I'm going to send the Earthmen right back to the Earth.

FIRST B.E.M. (*advancing with hand outstretched*): This is wonderful! How can I ever thank —

SHAM (*hastily*): Er – keep your distance, please. I don't want to stink of sulphur for the next week.

FIRST B.E.M. (*retreating*): Oh. Sorry, I'm sure. No offence.

SHAM: How soon can you send the Earthmen back to me?

FIRST B.E.M.: At twice the speed of light.

SHAM: That'll do. And now go away.

FIRST B.E.M.: With pleasure. What ho, lads, let's sing as we march, shall we?

Exit B.E.M.s, *gaily singing a marching song.*

SHAM (*advancing to the footlights, to the audience*): I only hope I'm doing the right thing.

Re-enter GIMBLE *with* SPIV.

GIMBLE: Here he is, guvnor.

SHAM: Ah, Spiv! I think I might have some business for you, after all.

SPIV: That's really handsome of you, Sham.

SHAM: Not at all. Got your samples ready?

SPIV: You bet!

SHAM: I think you're just about to make your fortune. Ah, here they come. Stand by.

Enter the three EARTHMEN.

FRANK: Hallo, you funny little things! (*Seeing Spiv.*) Good lord, there's another one of them!

SHAM: Good evening. Had a good time?

DICK: We've met your Bug-Eyed Monsters.

BILL: And taught them how civilized beings behave.

SHAM: Really? And what did they say?

FRANK: Oh, they were tremendously impressed. They're much more intelligent than you are, of course.

SHAM: Are they, indeed? How nice.

DICK: When we explained what life was like on the Earth, they were so ashamed that they crept away.

BILL: We're going to educate them. We're going to open schools all over Venus.

SHAM: What a good idea! But allow me to introduce a friend of mine. Earthmen – Spiv; Spiv – Earthmen.

FRANK: And who is this queer little fellow?

SHAM: Spiv's a scientist. He comes from Mercury.

BILL: A scientist. How amusing!

SHAM: Show them your wares, Spiv.

SPIV *brings forward his suitcase and opens it, while the* EARTHMEN *regard him with amusement, as visitors to the Zoo might watch the antics of a monkey.*

SPIV (*fishing out a piece of apparatus*): Well, gents, this is a death-ray. It'll wipe out a whole city.

The attitude of the Earthmen undergoes a perceptible change.

FRANK (*taking the death-ray in his hands and examining it closely*): I say . . . this really is brilliant.

DICK (*taking death-ray in his turn*): Civilization of the highest order!

The EARTHMEN *exchange an awkward glance.*

BILL: Er – please excuse us, sir, for being rude just now. We realize that you come from a really advanced planet.

SPIV: Well, now, this (*Producing another piece of apparatus*) is a disintegrator. It turns people's bodies to heaps of dust.

FRANK: Magnificent!

DICK: How humble it makes me feel, to meet a really first-class brain!

BILL: Don't interrupt. (*To Spiv*) Pray go on, sir.

SPIV: And this (*He produces a helmet-shaped object*) is an annihilation-cap. You just put it on, think, and the whole area falls to bits.

FRANK (*breathlessly*): Wonderful. Absolutely wonderful.

BILL: Vastly superior to anything we've got on Earth.

SHAM (*casually*): Spiv was thinking of visiting the Earth, as it happens.

SPIV: Oh, no, I —

SHAM: Sh-h!

FRANK: Really? What an honour for us!

DICK: All the universities will give him a degree.

BILL: He'll get the Nobel Prize!

SPIV: The Nobel Prize? What's that for?

SHAM: Peace.

SPIV (*rather bewildered*): Well, its very kind of you gents to offer me all these honours, but the point is, will I get any money, because you see —

FRANK: Money? My dear sir, on my planet we honour genius. You'll make an enormous fortune.

SPIV: Oh, well, in that case —

DICK: You'll come with us to the Earth?

SPIV: Why, yes, I'd be glad to.

FRANK: Splendid! What a great day for the World!

DICK: Look, fellows, let's forget about the B.E.M.s. This is so much more important.

BILL: But when can we start? Our space-ship's wrecked.

SPIV: You can come in mine, if you like. It's quite comfortable.

FRANK: May we? It's so very good of you.

DICK: When can we start?

SPIV: Well, now, if you like.

EARTHMEN (*together*): Yes, let's not waste a single minute!

GIMBLE: Aren't you going to eat your supper?

FRANK: Supper? We've no time for supper while genius waits. Come on, fellows, let's off to show the Earth these brilliant machines of death!

They pick up their space-helmets.

BILL (*bowing to Spiv*): You first, sir.

SPIV: No, no. After you. (*He waves Bill forward, and turns to Sham as the* EARTHMEN *exeunt.*) Sham, old friend – I don't know how to thank you!

SHAM: Oh, don't mention it. It's a pleasure.

Exit SPIV.

SHAM: Well, for once, everybody's happy. But for how long, I wonder?

GIMBLE: And they didn't even eat their supper!

SHAM: Well, you know what to do about that. Come on, I'm hungry.

They pick up the tray of food and go out as the

CURTAIN *falls*

You Never Heard Such Unearthly Laughter

A Psychic Phenomenon

CHARACTERS

THE GHOST OF THE DUKE
THE GHOST OF THE DUCHESS
THE GHOST OF THEIR SON GEOFFROY
THE GHOST OF THEIR DAUGHTER MATILDA
SIR BERT HIGGINS
LADY HIGGINS
ELSE, *their daughter*
SID, *their son*
THE WITCH

YOU NEVER HEARD SUCH UNEARTHLY
LAUGHTER

SCENE: *The hall of an ancient baronial castle. Two suits of armour,*
right centre and left centre, and 'tapestries' backstage through which
entrances may be made. Dim lighting. Enter MATILDA, *the ghost of a*
fourteenth-century wench, through the tapestries. Matilda died at the
age of sixteen, and has retained the pretty ways of that time of life. She
tiptoes forward, looks about her, darts backstage, slips through the
tapestries, and reappears instantly.

MATILDA: Incorporeal as I am, I should find this easy, and yet,
forsooth, the trick of it eludes me. (*Exit: reappears immediately.*)
No doubt it comes with practice. (*Exit: re-enter.*) Ha! I fancy
that was neater. I'll ... O! Mamma!
The DUCHESS *has entered, right.*

DUCHESS: Matilda!

MATILDA (*guiltily*): Mamma?

DUCHESS: Come here, child. (MATILDA *goes to her, reluctantly.*)
What was it I saw you doing?

MATILDA: Nothing of – of consequence, Mamma.

DUCHESS: Nothing? I thought I saw you disappearing and re-
appearing through the wall. (*Awkward silence.*) Come, was I
mistaken?

MATILDA: N-no, Mamma, you were not.

DUCHESS (*sorrowfully*): I was not, was I? Child, child, where did
you conceive such a barbaric vulgarity?

MATILDA: Mamma, the Witch —

DUCHESS: That beldame!

MATILDA: Yes, Mamma: she – she – the Witch told me that ghosts in
other parts of England make a regular practice of walking
through walls, and I thought —

DUCHESS: Child, what the rank and file does is no concern of ours. We are the ghosts of one of the oldest Medieval families. We cannot permit ourselves to be aware of ghosts in other parts of England. Socially, they do not exist. They have no past.

MATILDA: No, Mamma.

DUCHESS: Always remember: the modern ghost is a naïve post-Renaissance upstart without breeding. Doubtless the newly-rich find its presumption amusing, but those of truly noble blood are never diverted by buffoonery.

MATILDA: I don't think anyone finds them amusing, Mamma. The Witch says they like to frighten people. They clank chains, and groan, and carry their heads beneath their arms. People are terrified of them. Sometimes their hair turns white in a single night.

DUCHESS: Fie upon such antics! Come, what is it you should be?

MATILDA: 'A harmless phantom on its errands gliding,' Mamma.

DUCHESS: Quite so. 'An impalpable impression on the air; a sense of something moving to and fro.' How often have I not reminded you of this?

MATILDA: Yet being an impalpable impression does grow rather dull after five or six centuries, Mamma.

DUCHESS: It is better to be dull than vulgar, Matilda. (*Enter the* DUKE.) Ah, my lord! It would be well if you spoke severely to Matilda about the dangers of consorting with the Witch. The creature seems bent on filling the child's head with improprieties.

DUKE: The Witch? Ah, well, she's useful, my dear. She does bring us the news of the world every week. It is most cultural.

MATILDA: I wish she'd bring us someone to haunt.

DUCHESS (*proudly*): There has been no one worthy of this castle since the Duke and I were its owners, and FitzGilbert the Bloody slew us in our prime. It would be pleasant, of course, to have some noble family to haunt in a manner compatible with our station, but what family is there living who is worthy of this place?

Enter GEOFFROY, *a young gallant of eighteen.*

GEOFFROY: I say – I've just been talking to the Witch!

DUCHESS: Geoffroy, *really* – gliding in like the spectre of some Housecarl!

GEOFFROY: Sorry, Mother. But I say – the Witch —

DUCHESS: I wish that the Witch would reassume an earthly form. It is high time someone burned her again.

DUKE: You seem excited, Geoffroy, my boy. What has the Witch been telling you, eh?

GEOFFROY: She says that a new family is coming to live here!

DUKE   ⎫   Eh? What's that?
DUCHESS ⎬ (*together*):   A new family?
MATILDA ⎭   Oh, how exciting!

GEOFFROY: This is pukka gen. The Witch convoyed them down here, and —

DUKE: Geoffroy, I find this modern idiom beyond me. Please speak good plain Middle English.

GEOFFROY: Pardon, sire. A verray parfit gentil knight and his family are due to arrive here eftsoons.

DUKE: How eftsoons?

GEOFFROY: Almost at once. They're on their way now in one of those spivvy American cars with a mouth-organ front, and it was all the Witch could do to keep up with them, even with the old broomstick firing on all cylinders. She just managed to nose ahead of them in the final straight, though, because they got caught in a traffic jam, and —

DUCHESS: Geoffroy; I suppose all that means something, but I cannot imagine what. Do I understand that this nobleman and his family are to arrive here almost at once?

GEOFFROY: Yes!

DUCHESS: Well, it is splendid news. This knight may well have a thousand-year-old name.

DUKE: What *is* the name, Geoffroy, do you know?

GEOFFROY: Higgins, Sir Bert Higgins.

DUKE: It is not familiar to me.

DUCHESS: Yet methinks it is a name of great distinction. Higgins!

MATILDA: Verily, it rolleth well upon the tongue.

DUCHESS: Why, we shall now be able to do some refined haunting quite in keeping with our ancient pride. The situation is excellent.

MATILDA: No frightening, of course.

DUCHESS: It is unworthy, Matilda, even to mention such a thing.

GEOFFROY (*gazing off, right*): I say, they're here! They seem to be having trouble getting their car across ye drawbridge, gadzooks. They'll prang if they're not careful. That'd cause them a spot of wanhope, wouldn't it?

DUKE: Well, I only hope that when they're here you'll finally decide which century's English you're going to speak, my boy. Hobnobbing with the Witch has sadly confused your idiom.

DUCHESS: True. He cannot open his mouth without disgorging an anachronism.

GEOFFROY: Ah, they're across! . . . They're getting out of the car . . . By St Loy, they're an *extraordinary* looking crew!

DUCHESS: True nobility never looks ordinary.

GEOFFROY: All the same, I didn't expect it to look quite like this.

DUCHESS: Had we not better prepare to receive them?

DUKE: So soon? Do you think they altogether expect four medieval ghosts waiting for them in the hall?

DUCHESS: H'm – you say sooth, my lord. We had best render ourselves invisible, and watch them unobserved.

MATILDA: O yes – that will be fun!

DUKE: Yes. Now, how does one render oneself invisible? I've had the run of this place so long that I seem to have forgotten the trick of it.

MATILDA: Why, father – like this!

Black-out for a moment. When the lights return, Matilda has disappeared.

DUKE: Yes – you did that very neatly.

DUCHESS: Geoffroy! You next, please.

GEOFFROY: Very well, Mother. Bye-bye, everyone. I'll meet thee in that hollow vale.

Black-out procedure as before. Geoffroy vanishes.

DUCHESS: My lord?

DUKE: Ladies first, my dear.

DUCHESS: Very well. (*Black-out as before.*)
Voices outside.

DUKE: Ha, not much time. I hope this is going to work. Let me see . . . Ah! (*Black-out, etc.*)
Slightly brighter lighting. The four GHOSTS *reappear backstage, standing at intervals.*

DUCHESS: Matilda! Part of your person is showing.

MATILDA: Pardon, Mamma. (*Flicker of lights.*) Is that better?

DUCHESS: That will do.

GEOFFROY: Here they come!
Enter the HIGGINS FAMILY. *They are all expensively dressed in the height of bad taste.*

SIR BERT: Well, 'ere we are! Welcome, folks, to my ancestral habode!

LADY H: Cor, just like the real thing, ain't it?

SIR BERT: Watcher mean, just like it? It *is* the real thing, this is. Goes back to the twelfth century, this does.

ELSE (*who is about seventeen*): Coo – 'ow long is that, Dad?

SIR BERT: Couple of 'undred years at least.

SID (*about nineteen*): Like the blinking Chamber of 'Orrors, I reckon it is.

SIR BERT: Oh, go on! You'll get used to it, Sid boy. 'Ave a look round, now. There's plenty to see.
They wander about the hall.

DUKE: Is this person really a knight?

DUCHESS: Plainly not. These are wretched scullions sent on in advance to make the place habitable.

DUKE: I trust their lord will crop their ears when he arrives.

SIR BERT: Its 'ard to believe that this place actually belongs to me, ain't it?

DUKE: I say – did you note that?

LADY H: Well, you're a knight now, Bertie.

GEOFFROY: Pretty conclusive proof, what?

SID: That's right, Dad. All you want's a suit of armour. (*Taps one *of the suits of armour.*) And you've got even that! That's good, that is. Lovely bit of tin, this is.

DUKE: Confound the fellow! I used to joust in that suit!

SIR BERT *goes to where the Duke is standing, and leans against the wall, so that his outstretched arm is actually thrust through the arm of the Duke, who has his hand on his hip.*

SIR BERT: Yes, Sid, but you know what we *really* want in this castle, don't you?

SID: What's that, Dad?

SIR BERT: A ghost.

LADY H: Now then, father, don't be awful.

SIR BERT: I'm serious! Some old geezer wiv 'is 'ead under 'is arm...

DUKE: Of all the infernal impudence!

ELSE (*now standing beside Geoffroy*): Oh, no, Dad – an 'andsome young troubadour who died for love!

GEOFFROY: Rather a pretty thought, that.

SID: What about a sweet damsel in distress, wringing 'er 'ands? Blime, a sort of walking pin-up, she'd be.

MATILDA: Oh, go along with you! (*Blows lightly into his face.*)

DUCHESS: Matilda!!

MATILDA (*contritely*): Mamma.

SID: It's funny – I thought I felt a draught.

SIR BERT: Not 'ere you didn't, boy. Them walls is eight foot thick.

ELSE: Coo, Sid – perhaps it was the ghost.

LADY H: You be quiet now, Else. That sort of talk fair turns me stomach, it does. I wish we'd never bought this nasty place. It gives me the creeps.

SIR BERT: Oh, don't take on, Mother. Else was joking, wasn't you, duck? There's no such things as ghosts really.

The GHOSTS *exchange an indignant glance.*

LADY H: Do you mean that, Bertie?

SIR BERT: O' course.

LADY H: Well, I 'ope you're right. You know what I am – 'ypersensitive. It only takes a mouse or a spider to send cold shivers down me spine. I don't know what I'd do if I saw a ghost.

DUCHESS (*in a towering rage*): Madam, it would be a case of the supernatural meeting the subnormal!

MATILDA: She can't hear you, Mother.

SIR BERT: You don't want to worry, mother. I said the old castle could do with a ghost. I never said I believed in them myself. (*Advancing centre.*) I want the public to believe in 'em, though.

SID (*advancing centre*): Can't say I get you, quite.

SIR BERT (*jabbing him in the ribs*): Yer slow, Sid boy, yer slow. Don't the dear old public just love trooping round the Stately Homes of England at 'alf a crown a head? And won't they troop double-quick and twice as long if they think there's a genoo-ine ghost on the premises?

LADY H: Scare 'em off, most likely, it will.

SIR BERT: Be your age, mother. They'll love it. Morbid, they are.

ELSE: I'm beginning to see the light.

SID: Me too. You mean that you've rushed into buying this crazy place as a financial proposition?

SIR BERT: Too true I have. I 'aven't made a fortune and a knighthood out of selling old junk without recognizing a valuable heap of junk when I see it. When I think of the lolly that's lyin' dormant in this old castle, me 'ead swims. Look at all them rollin' acres outside – miles of fairground there, ain't there? Coconut-shies and side-shows all the year round, see? Then inside, a museum – oh yes, the public loves a bit o' culture – we'll shove all the junk we find in the castle into a couple o' rooms and get some Professor cove to label it all and write a booklet about it. All right, museum – entrance twopence —

SID: Make it sixpence.

SIR BERT: Too much, boy. Twopence is the limit for culture.

LADY H: But where does the ghost come in?

SIR BERT: Ah, yes. Conducted tour of the entire castle – at the public's own risk —

SID: Pretty touch, that.

SIR BERT: Thank you, boy – 'alf a crown a head for the conducted tour, with genoo-ine apparitions in every room likely to emerge and strike them dead with terror at any moment.

LADY H: They'll get a bit umpty if they don't see no ghosts, though, 'alf a crown apiece an' all.

SIR BERT: No, Mother. You just don't understand human nature. They'll make up their own ghost stories that fast that by the time this place has been open three weeks it'll have as many ghosts as a dog has fleas. That's the public for you. Neurotic, they are. There's real lolly in public neurosis if you know how to use it.

ELSE: Dad, you're a genius.

SIR BERT: That's my girl.

LADY H: Sounds all right, but where are we going to live?

SIR BERT: Ah, that's where I kill two birds with one stone, old dear. The East Wing. Stands apart in its own grounds, far from the maddin' crowd. We'll do it up lovely.

ELSE: Modernize it, I hope?

SIR BERT: Oh, sure. Private cinema, swimmin' pool, and so on.

DUCHESS: It was in the East Wing that FitzGilbert the Bloody surprised us, and I met with a fate worse than death.

MATILDA: Hush, Mother. It's no use being nostalgic.

SID: Well, it all sounds super, Dad. Let's go and see this 'ere East Wing now, shall we?

SIR BERT: Yes, all right. Come on, everyone. (*They begin to move left.*) Look out, mother, there's a ghost behind you! (LADY H *screams: exeunt protesting, the others laughing and chatting.*)
The GHOSTS *advance, centre.*

DUKE: Well, beshrew my soul!

GEOFFROY: A ghastly crew. Actually, I thought the girl less ghastly than the rest.

DUCHESS: Was that creature a girl? I should not have supposed it.

GEOFFROY: Oh, she was outstandingly feminine.

MATILDA: They were all deplorable, but if I had to choose one less deplorable than the others, I would choose the young man.

DUKE: What talk is this? Thumping my armour, not believing in ghosts, talking of trooping the rabble through my castle at half a crown a head? They shall not come here, and that's final.

DUCHESS: You say sooth, my lord, but —

DUKE: Final.

GEOFFROY: What you say, sire, may be sooth, but how are you going to stop them?

DUCHESS: Pause, my lord, and reflect. How, indeed, *are* we to prevent them coming here?

DUKE: What? Why, we shall – we shall — (*Baffled.*) Oh, confound it, we're helpless! Like rats in a trap.

MATILDA: Of course – forgive me, Mamma, if I displease you – we might *frighten* them away.

DUCHESS: Impossible, Matilda. Out of the question.

MATILDA: Then we shall have to put up with them. Indeed, for my part, I —

DUKE: Now wait a minute. What did you say, Matilda?

MATILDA: I said, we might frighten them away, Father.

DUKE: You know, that's quite an idea. That's quite an idea.

DUCHESS: Under no circumstances will I consent to play the ghoul.

GEOFFROY: If I may say so, Mother, you're missing the opportunity of a deathtime. You saw how easily they were ready to be frightened.

DUKE: Hang it, yes. We could send them scuttling out of here like scared rabbits.

MATILDA: It would be so easy.

GEOFFROY: And rather fun.

DUKE: Consider, my dear; do you not wish them to go?

DUCHESS: Vehemently.

DUKE: Then ponder on this.

DUCHESS: My lord – you lure me —

DUKE: Well, it's centuries since I've done that, anyway.

DUCHESS: And yet I fear that no good may come of it.

DUKE: Come, what possible harm can come of it? This frightening game – how does one set about it, do you know?

GEOFFROY: Well – poltergeists hurl things about —

DUKE: H'm – rather vulgar.

MATILDA: Some spectres re-enact some grisly scene in which they took part when living —

DUCHESS: I flatly refuse to re-enact my scene with FitzGilbert the Bloody.

GEOFFROY: It really isn't necessary. All a ghost has to do is – well, to appear.

DUKE: And that frightens people?

GEOFFROY: Yes.

DUKE: But why should it?

GEOFFROY: I suppose they scare easily.

DUKE: It sounds silly to me.

GEOFFROY: It has the advantage of being very little effort on the ghost's part. Shall we rehearse a little manifestation together?

DUKE: Yes – that might be a good idea.

MATILDA: Wait! I hear them coming back.

GEOFFROY: Then let's adjourn to the next room. This rehearsal requires privacy.

Exeunt GHOSTS. *Enter* HIGGINS FAMILY.

LADY H: Well, I only hope you 'aven't bought a pig in a poke, Bertie.

SIR BERT: Not a bit of it, me old duck. Tell you what, though – I think we ought to import a lot more junk for the museum – instruments of torture and that sort of thing. The public loves that. We don't want to spoil the ship for a 'aporth of tar.

SID: Yes, and I think we ought to import a ghost, too.

SIR BERT: Now don't talk fantastical, Sid.

SID: No, seriously, Dad. I'm thinking of what Mum said. If the public don't see something for their money sooner or later, they're going to cool off, imagination or not. It'll be easy enough – only a matter of mirrors and wires. Any conjurer would fix it up for you.

SIR BERT (*ruminating*): Yes – I see yer point, boy. We want some evidence of spookery, eh?

SID: That's it.

Enter the DUKE, *right.*

DUKE: In that case, may I offer you my services?

ELSE (*shrieking*): Dad – it's a *ghost*!

LADY H: O-o-oh – I can't stand it – take it away, take it away . . . (*Her voice gets fainter.*) Take it . . . O-o-o-oh! (*Swoons.*)

ELSE: She's fainted! *Do* something, can't you – Sid – Dad – *help*!

SIR BERT (*shaking with terror*): All right, now – all right – keep calm – it's a trick, I tell you – keep calm – it's a trick —

DUKE (*heartily*): No, no, my good sir, I'm quite genuine. Just step over here and put your arm right through me – or you, young fellow —

SID: Keep off me, willyer – go away —

DUKE (*advancing on Else*): – or you, my dear —

ELSE: Help! Help! Help!
Enter GEOFFROY.

GEOFFROY: Steady, Father, don't frighten the young lady too much. (*Going to her.*) Really, there's nothing to alarm you —

ELSE: Oh! Another one of them! O-o-o-oh! (*Swoons.*)

GEOFFROY: Gadzooks! Geoffroy the lady-killer!

DUKE: Come, my boy, with the women out of the way, we can *concentrate* on these two —

GEOFFROY: Yes, indeed. (*To Sid*) You, my fine fellow, have a nasty, pimply face. (*Waves arms menacingly.*)

DUKE (*to Sir Bert*): And you, sir, are a boor!
Enter MATILDA.

MATILDA: – and you're a horrid man who kills birds with stones!

SID: Dad – there's thousands of 'em – let's get out of here —

MATILDA: Pray, don't alarm yourself excessively — (*Takes his arm.*) Oh!
SID *has swooned.*

SIR BERT: Mum – Sid – Else – wake up, willyer! Don't leave me with a castle full of ghosts — (*He rushes right, to exit. Enter* DUCHESS, *in his path.*)

DUCHESS: Were you looking for a ghost, my man? Then gaze on me!

GEOFFROY: Congratulations, Mother – perfect entrance.

DUCHESS: Thank you, my son. I flatter myself I timed it nicely. (*Advancing.*) Come, don't cringe away like that. Let me enfold you in my spectral arms.

SIR BERT: No, lady, don't touch me – lemme get out of here —
  (*Looking desperately about.*)

DUKE: Guard the doors! Now, sir, you may leave if you dare!
  Which of us would you care to walk through?

DUCHESS: Come, let me embrace you! (SIR BERT *swoons.*) Why –
  what —?

MATILDA: He's fainted.

DUKE: Victory, by my halidom!

GEOFFROY: Down, down they go!

MATILDA: How magnificent! Mother, you were superb!

DUCHESS: Thank you, dear. You too haunted very prettily.

DUKE: All we need do now, I suppose, is to wait for them to re-
  cover and bolt for their lives.

GEOFFROY: Yes, a faint doesn't last long.

MATILDA: They seem – they seem to have swooned very profoundly, do they not?

DUKE: That's true. They're . . . very still.

GEOFFROY (*bending over Sid*): In fact, this one's stopped breathing.

MATILDA (*bending over Else*): And this one.

DUCHESS (*bending over Lady H*): And this!
  They stare at one another in growing apprehension. Enter WITCH.

WITCH: Well, well, well, you've made a pretty mess of things
  between you, haven't you? You know what you've been and
  gone and done?

DUCHESS: My good woman, what are you saying?

WITCH: No, Duchess, I'm a bad woman, and proud of it.

DUCHESS: But does this mean —?

WITCH: It certainly does.

DUCHESS: You're sure?

WITCH: Positive.

DUCHESS: O, horror, horror, horror!

DUKE (*impatiently*): Come, will you please stop talking in riddles?
  Whatever is this all about?

WITCH: It means you've got the Higgins crew as permanent
  guests, Duke, and may you enjoy it! They'll be all over the
  place, upstairs, downstairs, *and* in my lady's chamber, if I'm a
  judge of young Sid; and they won't stop at that, either. Refined

haunting, ha ha! They'll yoo-hoo like owls from the battle-
ments – they'll go larking through the grounds – they'll jump
out on people from behind trees in the lanes. You've got a
very vulgar lot of ghosts on your hands, Duke – too blooming
post-Renaissance for words. And before you can say Geoffrey
Chaucer you'll have the Psychical Researchers and cranks and
crackpots from the land of the living pouring into the castle
to investigate you. You've got it coming, and no mistake.

DUKE: I still don't understand —

DUCHESS: Oh don't be so irritatingly obtuse, my lord —

GEOFFROY: Wait! They're stirring.

The HIGGINS FAMILY *slowly and dazedly sit up. They gaze upon
the ghosts, puzzled, but without fear.*

SIR BERT: Where are we? Who are you lot? I seem to remember
you, vaguely like . . .

DUCHESS: Don't strain yourself to remember, sir. You have a
great deal of time before you in which to perfect our acquain-
tance. We frightened you all to death ten minutes ago.

SLOW CURTAIN

The Cinderella Story

An Unauthorized Version

CHARACTERS

THE PRESSMAN
THE QUEEN'S SECRETARY
LAVINIA ⎱ *the Ugly Sisters*
HONORIA ⎰
CINDERELLA
THE GODMOTHER
THE BARONESS
THE PRINCE
PRESS PHOTOGRAPHERS

THE CINDERELLA STORY

PROLOGUE

SCENE: *A room in the Queen's Palace in the Kingdom of Sudonia. This scene should be played against a background of curtains, so that there is as little delay as possible between the Prologue and the Act. It may be furnished at the Producer's discretion, and should resemble a waiting-room, with a settee and armchairs, etc., plus a small table bearing a telephone, right.*

The PRESSMAN *is seated in one of the armchairs, turning over the pages of a magazine. Middle-aged, experienced in his profession, he is nevertheless slightly overawed by the occasion, and is a little nervous.*

The QUEEN'S SECRETARY *enters, left.* PRESSMAN *rises hopefully. The Secretary is elderly, angular, and dignified to the point of severity. She conveys infinite condescension in her every speech.*

SECRETARY: I am sorry, the Queen is still resting. I doubt whether she will be able to see you for some little while yet.

PRESSMAN: I hope I may wait?

SECRETARY: Certainly: Her Majesty is always pleased to receive foreign journalists, especially those from a country as highly esteemed by Her Majesty as your own. She has instructed me to offer you some refreshment. Would that be acceptable?

PRESSMAN: Thank you – most kind – but I won't put you to that trouble. I dined well at the airport. Er – you did say I might use your phone —

SECRETARY: Of course: please do so whenever you like.

PRESSMAN: Thank you: I'm greatly obliged. I'll do so right away. (*Nervously talkative.*) I haven't seen much of Sudonia so far, naturally, but believe me I'm already deeply impressed with the way the personality of the fabulous Queen Cinderella dominates your country. A wonderful old lady, ma'am – I speak respectfully – a very wonderful old lady. Those great pictures of her in every square – they cry out to the foreign visitor of the love and devotion of your nation.

SECRETARY (*with the slightest trace of irony*): Yes. They are calculated so to do.

PRESSMAN: To be sure – a token to a royal lady who has long been a beautiful legend. I would like to say as much to my paper. And – would it be presuming too much, ma'am, to ask if *you* have any personal reminiscences of the Queen which I might quote? You have been her secretary for so long —

SECRETARY: I am afraid I cannot do that. Her Majesty has servants: she does not have them interviewed.

PRESSMAN: I'm sorry – I meant no offence.

SECRETARY (*less coldly*): Please don't apologize. The request was natural. I'm sorry I can't grant it. (*After a slight pause.*) The Queen likes to make personally all statements to the Press which concern herself. She is thus in less danger of being . . . misrepresented.

PRESSMAN: Ah . . . Very wise.

SECRETARY (*dryly*): It is indeed. And now if you will excuse me, I will leave you to your telephone call. I will return as soon as ever Her Majesty is pleased to receive you.

PRESSMAN: Thank you very much indeed, ma'am. (*Exit* SECRETARY. *He goes to phone.*) Operator – I want an overseas call, please, to the Republic of Erstwile . . . thanks . . . Hallo? . . . Yes, please, I want Mayhem 4747 . . . Yes, I'll hold on . . .

Enter LAVINIA. *She is a white-haired, sweet old lady of sixty-nine.*

LAVINIA (*in an excited whisper*): Honoria! It's him! Come quickly!

HONORIA (*in a fruity contralto, off*): Good! I'm coming.

Enter HONORIA. *Seventy-one, she is stouter and redder-faced than Lavinia, but yet a handsome woman.*

PRESSMAN (*at phone*): Hallo? . . . Yes, it's me all right. Yes, I'm right inside the palace. I want a stenographer – Millie for preference . . . Ah, Millie? . . . You know who's speaking, don't you? . . . Well, look, I haven't seen Queen Cinderella yet, and it may be some time before I do, so we'll put in a column about Sudonia Celebrates Cinderella's Anniversary . . . Am I impressed? I was never so moved in my life . . . No, really, I'm serious – these huge crowds – all so happy, all re-joicing . . . You wish you were here? All right, I'll bring you next time . . . What? Oh, well, naturally, I'll bring my wife as well . . . Yes, all right, dear, but this is an expensive call: let's get to work, shall we? Ready? Good . . .

He sees the sisters, who are by now on either side of him.

– No, wait a bit, Millie – I think I'm summoned. I'll call you back —

LAVINIA: No – no – do go on —

PRESSMAN: Millie! – Millie! . . . Oh, she's rung off.

LAVINIA: Oh, I am sorry. That was our fault, I'm afraid.

PRESSMAN: It's of no consequence, I assure you. Did you ladies wish to speak to me?

LAVINIA (*with a glance at her sister*): Well, as a matter of fact we did – but we'd get into dreadful trouble if anyone found out.

HONORIA: We're going to risk that. I believe you are a journalist, sir?

PRESSMAN: Yes, from the *Erstwile Daily World.*

HONORIA: Well, the *Erstwile Daily World* can have the story of a lifetime straight from the horse's mouth, if you care to hear it.

PRESSMAN: That's generous of you, ma'am, but to whom have I the honour of speaking?

LAVINIA: We, sir, are the legitimate daughters of Cinderella's stepmother.

PRESSMAN: The daughters – but, I say, that means you must be —

LAVINIA (*gently*): Well? What must we be?

PRESSMAN: Well – excuse me, but – the Ugly Sisters!

HONORIA: Quite right. We're the Ugly Sisters – fifty years older now, and a bit shop-soiled.

PRESSMAN: But, really – you embarrass me, ladies —

HONORIA: It's been embarrassing for us, too, being called Ugly all our lives. Rather discouraging to any possible beau, you know.

PRESSMAN: But this is amazing! You are not ugly – in fact, if I may say so —

HONORIA: Oh, don't bother, we're past caring. All the same, you've learned something new – the Ugly Sisters aren't ugly. And fifty years ago we were even less so – I was a bit hefty, but a healthy specimen, and Lavinia here was a sweetheart. The prince was crazy about her.

PRESSMAN: Who? The late King, you mean?

LAVINIA: That's right. The one who married Cinderella.

PRESSMAN: He was in actual fact in love with you?

LAVINIA: He said he was, and I've never had reason to doubt his word.

PRESSMAN: Then why —?

LAVINIA: Ah, it's a long story.

PRESSMAN: It must be. Very different from the one that's gone round the world all these years.

LAVINIA: Round the world? So far, really?

PRESSMAN: Yes, indeed. It's even reached Britain.

HONORIA: Britain?

PRESSMAN: A small island off the coasts of Europe.

HONORIA: Never heard of it.

PRESSMAN: Dreadful place – the natives charge at one another in chariots with knives sticking out of the wheels, I'm told – but even they have their own primitive version of the Cinderella legend.

LAVINIA: The Authorized Version.

PRESSMAN: There's only one legend, to my knowledge.

HONORIA: That's just it. We never leave this palace. We've seen many journalists here, but we've never been able to get at them before. Been past caring, too. No use raking up old scores. But now that we're in sight of the grave —

PRESSMAN: Come, come —

LAVINIA: Honoria's right. She's seventy-one and I'm sixty-nine. That doesn't leave us so long.

HONORIA: Now, as I say, we realize that our time's running out, we feel that we must tell the truth to someone.

LAVINIA: You will listen, won't you?

PRESSMAN: Of course I'll listen, but —

LAVINIA: That is nice of you. We love talking. Well, now, you must imagine that we are fifty years younger – not much more than girls —

The lights fade slowly.

HONORIA (*removing her grey wig*): Our hair wasn't grey – mine was brown —

LAVINIA (*removing her wig*): – mine was golden —

HONORIA (*removing her housecoat*): Our clothes were in the height of fashion —

LAVINIA (*removing her housecoat*): – That they were —

PRESSMAN: Yes?

LAVINIA: Well, now – one morning I came into the kitchen – Cinderella sitting in the fireplace, as usual – moping —

SLOW CURTAIN

SCENE TWO

The Baroness's kitchen. CINDERELLA, *in rags, huddles in the chimney-corner, right. She is a slight, pretty girl, with great wistful eyes. Her normal expression is petulant, but she can resort to spaniel-like pathos when necessary.*

Enter LAVINIA. *Not seeing Cinderella, she goes cautiously to the door and peeps out.*

CINDERELLA: Your shoes are under the table, Lavinia.

LAVINIA (*starting violently*): Oh! Cinders, you startled me. I didn't see you.

CINDERELLA: Your shoes – they're under the table.

LAVINIA (*a trifle bewildered*): My shoes? Oh, yes, so they are.

CINDERELLA: I've cleaned them for you.

LAVINIA: Oh. Oh yes, so you have. Well, thanks. It really wasn't necessary, you know – but still, thanks.

CINDERELLA: And what do you wish me to do for you now?

LAVINIA: Do? Nothing.

CINDERELLA: Yes, yes, you must let me serve you.

LAVINIA: Cinders, please don't talk like that. It makes one feel awkward. Why ever should you keep doing things for me? I'm perfectly capable of looking after myself.

CINDERELLA: You know that my position here —

LAVINIA: Now, look here. You know jolly well that Mother, with her desperate longing to be strictly fair, has always favoured you just because you're *not* her daughter, so for goodness' sake don't talk such rubbish.

CINDERELLA: Abuse me, go on: I can't defend myself.

LAVINIA: Oh — ! Cinders, I honestly believe you're ill. Mentally ill, I mean. No one normal would behave as you do – dressing like that when you've got a trunkful of decent frocks upstairs, and acting the poor little slavey to everyone's embarrassment. Don't you think you might have a – a persecution complex, or something? We're studying that sort of thing at college now, and I assure you that some people —

CINDERELLA: It isn't kind, frightening me with terms I can't understand – taking advantage of your superior education. I don't go to college —

LAVINIA (*angrily*): And why not? Because you played the little ninny at school, that's why, and funked all your exams pretending to be ill.

CINDERELLA: I see. I was pretending then, but now, to suit your convenience, I'm really ill.

LAVINIA: You're deliberately twisting my words, you know you are!

CINDERELLA: I'm afraid I'm not clever enough to follow that, Lavinia dear. Perhaps if I had the advantages of a higher education —

LAVINIA: Perhaps then you'd see what a beastly little *poseuse* you are!

CINDERELLA: How valuable! And I'd meet all kinds of interesting people, too, wouldn't I? Rich ones, too, and great – like the Prince.

LAVINIA: You leave the Prince out of this!

CINDERELLA: Oh yes, of course – I shouldn't have mentioned him, should I? As his fellow-undergraduate, I suppose you have a major claim to him?

LAVINIA: How dare you! How dare you!

CINDERELLA: Oh, I'm sorry if I've touched a tender spot. I should have known why you were looking so anxiously out of that door. We're expecting a royal visit, are we?

LAVINIA: We, my good Cinderella, are expecting nothing. What I may do is my own business.

CINDERELLA (*by now wholly venomous*): But mightn't it be a little awkward, doing your billing and cooing with your ragged poor relation huddling in the cinders, watching you? I'm sure the Prince wouldn't approve. They tell me he's a very idealistic young man, and an ardent social reformer.

The GODMOTHER, *unseen by Lavinia, but seen by Cinderella enters.* CINDERELLA *immediately changes her tone to one of meek submissiveness.*

LAVINIA: Why, you rotten little bitch!

CINDERELLA: Please, dear sister, don't abuse me so.

LAVINIA: Oh, for Heaven's sake don't go back on that tack again. Abuse you! If you dare open your mouth again I – I'll take that ridiculous broom of yours and break it over your head.

CINDERELLA (*piteously*): Oh, no, no! Oh won't someone help me please?

GODMOTHER (*stepping forward*): Don't be frightened, my darling. (*Both girls start, Lavinia in genuine, Cinderella in feigned surprise. To Lavinia.*) Ah, you didn't expect me to come in through the kitchen, did you, miss? Yes, you may well blush, my girl. I heard what you were saying. A fine way to speak to your sister!

LAVINIA: Godmother – you don't understand —

GODMOTHER: I think I can understand what I hear with my own ears, Lavinia. I never heard anything like it in my life – cursing like a harridan and threatening the child with violence —

CINDERELLA: Please, Godmother, I don't think dear Lavinia quite knew what she was saying.

LAVINIA: I jolly well did.

GODMOTHER: Indeed! Cinderella, my poor sweet forgiving lamb, what can you know of the Seven Deadly Sins? You know to which sin I refer, Lavinia? Wrath, my girl, wrath – yes, and Pride and Envy too, I'll be bound. Well, you're not too big for me to give you a good smacking, my lady, so take care!

LAVINIA (*beside herself with fury*): You try it, that's all! You damned well try it!

Enter BARONESS: *matronly, charming, competent.*

BARONESS: Whatever is this commotion all about?

GODMOTHER: Ask Lavinia. She has so far cursed and sworn like a navvy at both myself and this poor child, and has threatened both of us with violence.

BARONESS: Oh, Lavinia, really —

GODMOTHER: 'Oh, Lavinia, really!' I know what I'd do if she were my child.

LAVINIA: Mother, please —

BARONESS (*mildly*): Lavinia, it's always silly to lose your temper. It puts you in the wrong whether you're there or not. And that scene I overheard was rather vulgar, wasn't it?

LAVINIA: I'm sorry, Mother. (*She begins to leave kitchen.*)

CINDERELLA (*sweetly*): Lavinia, dear, do take your shoes. I've cleaned them for you.

LAVINIA: In that case I wouldn't be seen dead in them. (*Exit.*)

GODMOTHER: Oh! You saw that? Is there no way this poor little thing can appease the vixen? Why, it's pathetic!

BARONESS: Yes, very. Cinderella, why exactly did you clean Lavinia's shoes? Buttons would have done them for her, if she'd wanted him to. After all, we pay him for that sort of thing.

CINDERELLA: No, no, Stepmother, I wouldn't like to give any more work to dear, faithful Buttons.

BARONESS: Dear, faithful Buttons has a cushy job here, and well you know it. But in any case, I'm sure Lavinia would clean her own shoes, if necessary. She's not lazy, to my knowledge.

And now, Cinders, my dear, I want you to do something for me.

CINDERELLA (*jumping up*): Certainly, Stepmother dear!

GODMOTHER: I hope you're not overworking the child, Letitia!

BARONESS: I hope that you will allow me to run my own family, Lysistrata. (*To Cinderella*) It's just this – will you please go upstairs and change into some respectable clothes? Those you have on are a disgrace.

CINDERELLA (*with some reluctance*): If you wish it, Stepmother.

BARONESS: Of course I wish it. You look like a tramp. Run along, now.

GODMOTHER: Come, my darling, I'll help you choose your dress. If I'm allowed to, of course.

BARONESS: Of course, of course. (*Exeunt* GODMOTHER *and* CINDERELLA.) And perhaps you might choose a nice windowsill and throw yourself off it. (*Sighing.*) Oh, dear, *families!* *Enter* HONORIA.

Hallo, dear. How did the hockey practice go?

HONORIA: Well, the new lot are just about as bad as they could be, without being actually armless or legless. I came in this way because my shoes are filthy.

BARONESS: Are they? Well, will you please clean them as soon as possible?

HONORIA: Yes, all right. Why?

BARONESS: If you don't, Cinderella will probably decide to serve you, as she puts it, by cleaning them for you, and I want to avoid that.

HONORIA: Oh, Lord! is she still playing that game?

BARONESS: She is.

HONORIA: I wonder what she's up to? Perhaps she's a bootfetichist.

BARONESS: You psychology students! Whatever's a boot-whatever-you-said?

HONORIA: Boot-fetichist. Well, it's a person who craves to clean other people's shoes, owing to a morbid affliction of the nerves – nearly always sexual. A perversion, in popular terminology.

BARONESS: Oh, I see. No, I don't think Cinderella's one of those.

HONORIA: Some sort of exhibitionist, anyway.

BARONESS: Yes, she was exhibiting altogether too much in those awful rags she put on this morning. I sent her to change. I wish I knew what she's up to.

A knock at the door.

HONORIA: That'll be Buster.

BARONESS: Do you mean the Prince?

HONORIA: Yes. He's come for Lavinia. (*Calling at Wings left.*) Lavinia! he's here!

BARONESS (*as the knock is repeated*): Let him wait. This friendship worries me. The daughter of a minor Baron is never going to make a Queen, and I don't want my girl's heart broken.

HONORIA: Oh, they're just good pals.

BARONESS: Oh! Don't they teach you about *people* at that college? (*Enter* LAVINIA.)

HONORIA (*to Lavinia*): He's arrived. (*Heavy knocking.*) I say, your eyes are all red.

LAVINIA: Hay fever.

HONORIA (*doubtfully*): Rotten luck, old girl. (*Exeunt* HONORIA *and* BARONESS.)

LAVINIA *opens door.*

PRINCE (*entering*): Hallo, darling! I thought you were all out. (*Taking her shoulders.*) Hey, what's this? Have you been crying?

LAVINIA: No.

PRINCE: Yes, you have. What's upset you? The sweet little step-sister again?

LAVINIA: Yes.

PRINCE: What complex has she got now?

LAVINIA: I don't know. She's taken to dressing in rags.

PRINCE: Go on? A form of masochism, perhaps?

LAVINIA: She just likes drawing attention to herself.

PRINCE: Well, forget her. (*Taking her in his arms.*) I have sensational news —

LAVINIA (*repulsing him*): No, Buster. No, don't.

PRINCE: What's this? You really *are* upset, aren't you?

LAVINIA: Buster, I've got to talk seriously to you. I know we're just good friends and there's nothing in it and all that, but I'm a human being, and I just can't —

PRINCE: Who says there's nothing in it? (*Pause.*) Who are just good friends? I love you. Is that clear? I love you, and want to marry you.

LAVINIA: Don't be an idiot.

PRINCE: Now look here —

LAVINIA: You're so irresponsible! How long do you think this – this charade of being an ordinary college boy is going to last? You're the future king, Buster; you know jolly well you can't marry me. You'll marry royalty and settle down to producing sons and heirs. They won't be my children! They won't be mine!

PRINCE: Ah, but —

LAVINIA: No, I'll be lucky to be one of Her Majesty's ladies-in-waiting. Ha, I'll lace her beastly stays so tight she'll go black in the face! Or does a lady-in-waiting do that sort of thing?

PRINCE: May I please get a word in edgeways?

LAVINIA (*subdued*): Sorry.

PRINCE: Will you please listen carefully while I speak in words of one syllable? I'm going to marry you – if you'll have me.

LAVINIA: Oh, Buster, darling.

PRINCE: It's like this. My father's a democrat. That's why I'm an irresponsible student at a public university. He wants a grandchild; he's getting on, you know. So – I must get married. We're agreed that's essential. A State-arranged marriage with foreign royalty? Not a bit of it. Father's a democrat and a patriot.

LAVINIA: Well?

PRINCE: Well: he proposes to hold a Royal Ball which any girl in the kingdom may attend, and to marry me to the one I dance with the most.

LAVINIA (*laughing in spite of herself*): Oh, but that's preposterous! How many million girls do you expect to entertain?

PRINCE: Ah, his democratic spirit is well in check, really. No one of rank lower than a Baronetcy may attend.

LAVINIA: Oh.

PRINCE: But that let's you in, doesn't it?

LAVINIA (*breathlessly*): When is this ball, Buster?

PRINCE: Any week now. I'm going to dance with you so persistently that they'll take us for Siamese twins.

LAVINIA: Oh! – Oh! no, it's too good to be true. . . . Darling, I'm going to cry.

PRINCE (*tenderly*): What, again? You're not one of these weepy women, I hope? A Queen must wear a smile, you know.

LAVINIA: Don't make fun, Buster, not now.

PRINCE: Where is your mother? I want to tell her about this. I have a feeling she doesn't trust me, and I'd like my future mother-in-law to know I'm on the square.

LAVINIA: Ought you to? I mean, are you absolutely certain about it, Buster? Because —

PRINCE: Of course, of course I'm certain. Where is she?

LAVINIA: Somewhere in the house.

PRINCE: Come on, then. I mustn't stay long, or the blasted newspaper men will track me here, and I don't want that to happen. Mustn't let it be thought that my democratic marriage is a frame-up.

LAVINIA: Slip out through the kitchen again.

PRINCE: Yes, I will. Come on. (*Exeunt both.*)

Slight pause. Enter GODMOTHER *and* CINDERELLA, *who is wearing a pretty frock.*

GODMOTHER: Now, don't you let them force you into that nasty chimney-corner again, my darling.

CINDERELLA: I'm afraid they will, Godmother dear. They'll make me take this frock off, too. Stepmother only told me to put it on to impress you.

GODMOTHER: Oh, you poor, poor child. Is there nothing I can do to help you?

CINDERELLA: Just one tiny thing, dear Godmother.

Her voice, though still meek, has a note of purpose which the Godmother has never heard before.

GODMOTHER (*curiously*): And what is it, my love?

CINDERELLA: Will you please go out and collect as many Press photographers as you can, and bring them here?

GODMOTHER: But, my darling, really – what a strange request!

CINDERELLA (*sweetly, but with significance*): The Prince is in this house, Godmother, dear.

GODMOTHER (*after a longish pause*): Cinderella —

CINDERELLA: Yes?

GODMOTHER: If – if you should ever find yourself . . . in a suddenly exalted position . . . my dearest girl . . . you wouldn't forget your old Godmother, would you, pet?

CINDERELLA (*steadily*): If ever that happened – she would also be in an exalted position, dearest Godmother.

GODMOTHER (*decisively*): I'll do what you wish at once.

CINDERELLA (*as* GODMOTHER *turns to go*): – and, Godmother, dear! When you return, will you ring the front door bell, and then bring the photographers round here to the kitchen as soon as you can?

GODMOTHER: I will, my darling. (*Exit.*)

CINDERELLA (*hard as nails*): And don't bungle it, you old cow.

Enter PRINCE.

CINDERELLA (*sinking to the floor in a curtsy*): Your Highness.

PRINCE (*coolly*): Hallo, Cinderella. Don't do that, it's not neces-sary. Excuse me, won't you. I'm just off.

CINDERELLA: Of course, your Highness. The photographers are waiting for you.

PRINCE (*startled*): Are they? Where?

CINDERELLA: Outside.

PRINCE: Hell! Do they know I'm here?

CINDERELLA: I don't think they're certain, your Highness. They seem to be just hanging about in hope.

PRINCE: Fools! Have they nothing better to do? Well, they mustn't see me, that's certain. If you'll allow me, I'll wait here for a while.

CINDERELLA: Of course, your Highness. Please sit down. I'll go back to my chimney-corner, out of your way.

PRINCE: But — (*Curiously.*) I say, must you? There seem to be plenty of chairs to sit on.

CINDERELLA: I belong in the chimney-corner, your Highness. It is my place.

PRINCE: How peculiar. Won't that nice dress get dirty?

CINDERELLA: This dress? Oh, it's not *me*, this dress – just disguise for the poor thing I am. I'll take it off.
Pulls dress over her head.

PRINCE (*alarmed*): Here – steady —

CINDERELLA (*now seen to be wearing her rags underneath*): There, your Highness. I'm now dressed as I ought to be – in my rags.

PRINCE (*sharply*): But why on earth should you be? No one wants you to. Why do you carry on like this?
CINDERELLA *stares piteously at him for several moments. She then speaks with a startling change of tone.*

CINDERELLA: Oh, you're right, you're right! (*Throwing herself into a chair, burying her head in her arms.*) I'm a beastly little *poseuse*, that's what I am! I hate myself! (*Sobbing.*) I hate myself!

PRINCE (*troubled*): Oh, please, don't distress yourself – I'm sorry —

CINDERELLA (*passionately*): No, no, you're right! I just act like this to upset everyone, and I hate myself for it! They're all so good to me here – Stepmother – the girls – especially Lavinia, she's sweet to me – and this is how I repay them! I hate myself!

PRINCE: Well, that's hard luck, but surely you can stop it if you want to, can't you?

CINDERELLA: That's just it, I can't! Haven't you heard of cases like mine? You're a psychologist – a brilliant student —

PRINCE: I'm not, you know. I'll be lucky to get a third-class.

CINDERELLA: Still, you know all about psychology. Don't you think I might have a – a – persecution complex, or something?

PRINCE: Well, yes, that's possible.

CINDERELLA: Then will you please, please tell me how to lose it?

PRINCE: I'm afraid I can't. We're still doing theory; haven't tackled therapy yet. Honoria might help. She's done therapy.

CINDERELLA: Ah, no: my relationship with Honoria is too subjective. You *do* see that?

PRINCE: I see your point. Well, you could come to see us at the college.

CINDERELLA: And be pulled about by all the students? I should be even more maladjusted than ever.

PRINCE: Well, I don't know ... Do you have any dreams? We're just doing dreams.

CINDERELLA: Dreams? Oh yes. Full of strange symbols.

PRINCE: That's the ticket. Tell me one.

CINDERELLA: I'm sitting in the chimney-corner, and there are mice playing round my feet. There's a huge pumpkin on the table —

PRINCE (*soberly*): Significant. That's significant.

CINDERELLA: Yes. Morbid, isn't it?

PRINCE: Very. Go on.

CINDERELLA: The house is empty. My sisters and Stepmother have gone off to a Ball, laughing and jeering at me because I must stay at home in my rags. I am weeping. Suddenly my Godmother appears before me —

PRINCE: Ah! Haggish? A figure of horror?

CINDERELLA: Funnily enough, no. She comes as a Fairy, beautiful and radiant.

PRINCE: But still recognizable?

CINDERELLA: Yes.

PRINCE: A miracle of the Unconscious Mind.

CINDERELLA: She smiles, and waves her wand. Everything is transformed! I'm wearing a superb evening gown, and glass slippers: the mice turn into horses, and the pumpkin into a magnificent golden coach, which positively fills the room. There are some frogs that turn into coachmen. And there it is, my coach and four, ready to take me to the Ball —

PRINCE: How do you get it out of the kitchen?

CINDERELLA (*just a little impatiently*): Oh, really, I don't know. This is a dream, you know. Anyway, I'm taken to the Ball, and all evening I'm dancing with a rich, handsome young man. He is in love with me. We dance and dance; then we sit one out; he takes my hand; passion rises —

PRINCE: I say. Yes?

CINDERELLA: Then the clock strikes twelve.

PRINCE (*disappointed*): Oh. Does that matter?

CINDERELLA: Yes, it seems very important. I'm seized with panic. I jump up and run away, and then I'm running, running back home in my rags, with one glass slipper missing . . . and then I wake up.

PRINCE: H'm. The symbol of the shoe is very persistent, isn't it?

CINDERELLA: Yes. I'm waiting for the shoe to be on the other foot.

PRINCE: I'm not sure I follow that.

CINDERELLA: I hope you will, in time.

PRINCE: Well, let's think about this. My analysis, I think, would be that yours is a case of wish fulfilment, strongly enforced with inferiority-complex.

CINDERELLA: Marvellous! But the cure, your Highness? The treatment?

PRINCE: You've got me there.

CINDERELLA: Hypnosis, do you think?

PRINCE: Perhaps.

CINDERELLA: Can you hypnotize people?

PRINCE: I've never tried. I've seen it done.

CINDERELLA: How is it done?

PRINCE: Oh, well, the hypnotist stares into the patient's eyes – like this – and repeats some phrase over and over again, you know, like, 'You're going to sleep and forget, sleep and forget, sleep and forget' – see?

CINDERELLA (*drowsily*): I see.

PRINCE: Mind you, it takes an expert to bring it off . . . (*With sudden alarm.*) Here, are you all right? (*Snaps fingers before her face.*) Cinderella! Cinderella, wake up! Good Lord, I haven't the faintest idea how to get you out of this! Cinderella! Stand up! Snap out of it! (CINDERELLA *rises, arms outstretched, as if sleep-*

walking, and advances upon him.) Shades of the Sorcerer's Apprentice! (*Dodging round table.*) Whoever would have thought you'd drop off as easily as that!

Sound of the front door bell. CINDERELLA *quickens her pace.*

Cinderella - there's someone coming - please wake up!

He takes her shoulders and shakes her, gingerly. She responds by wrapping him tightly in her arms. As this happens, the door opens, and the GODMOTHER *enters with a crowd of Press photographers. There should be as many of these as possible.*

CINDERELLA: Of course I'll marry you - *darling!*

Kisses him on the mouth. The photographers, uttering cries of joy, are taking pictures from every conceivable angle.

GODMOTHER (*Sinking into a low curtsy*): Oh, your Highness! Oh, Cinderella, my dear, my very dear girl!

Enter BARONESS, HONORIA, *and* LAVINIA.

BARONESS	What in the name of goodness —
HONORIA (*together*):	Well, I'm dashed —
LAVINIA	Buster!!!

PRINCE (*over Cinderella's shoulder*): Now look here, I can explain everything —

A PHOTOGRAPHER: Please, your Highness. Your story!

General eager chorus from photographers.

PRINCE (*wildly, wrestling with Cinderella*): Get out! Get out, you lot!

PHOTOGRAPHER: Yes, your Highness! At once, your Highness! Come on, fellows, we've got the pictures!

GODMOTHER (*shepherding them out*): I'll tell you everything, gentlemen - the whole romance, from start to finish!

PRINCE: Don't you say anything, d'you hear? Don't you —

LAVINIA (*grieved and furious*): Isn't it rather late to start shouting now?

PRINCE: Late? Shouting? Are you all mad here? Can't anyone pull this - this psychopath off me?

CINDERELLA: *Darling!*

LAVINIA (*struggling with her*): Let him go! Let him go!

HONORIA: Steady on, old girl! I mean to say —

BARONESS (*imperiously*): Be quiet! Be quiet, all of you!

Abrupt silence. CINDERELLA *releases Prince, who sinks to the floor.*

Now, your Highness: you have, you say, something to explain to us?

PRINCE (*temporarily unhinged*): Yes. She went for a ride in a pumpkin —

HONORIA: Is this a limerick or something?

PRINCE: – drawn by mice —

LAVINIA (*to Cinderella, furiously*): He's gone mad! What have you done to him?

PRINCE: – one glass slipper – very significant —

LAVINIA (*sobbing*): He's mad! He's mad!

PRINCE (*with a burst of anger*): I'm not mad, confound you!

PRINCE ⎫
HONORIA ⎬ (*together*):
BARONESS ⎪
LAVINIA ⎭

Will you listen —
Steady, old girl,
I can't make head or tail of —
Stop saying 'steady old girl' —!

Sudden silence.

CINDERELLA (*sweetly poisonous*): I think, you know, you'd all better listen to me.

Silence again.

In fact, unless I'm much mistaken, you're all going to be listening to me from now on. The shoe's on the other foot, your Highness; do you follow me? on the other foot . . .

SLOW CURTAIN

EPILOGUE

SCENE: *as in Prologue. Pressman, Lavinia, Honoria, discovered.*

LAVINIA: – well, that's not the whole story, but it was the beginning of the end. Pictures of Cinderella embracing the

Prince appeared in every paper in the kingdom, and what was described as 'the full story' filled them all.

HONORIA: They differed from paper to paper, the stories.

LAVINIA: Yes, but they all made the same point: the Prince was going to marry Cinderella.

PRESSMAN: But what did the Prince have to say?

HONORIA: What did his father have to say! He nearly had apoplexy.

LAVINIA: Yes, he talked of banishing us all, and the Prince with us. It was an anxious period for Cinderella. Then she got an audience with him.

PRESSMAN: And talked him round?

LAVINIA: In about ten minutes. We'd underrated her, you know. What a saleswoman!

PRESSMAN: True. She's sold herself to the whole world.

LAVINIA: Anyway, the King was charmed with her. Called her his little daughter, and said that no son of his was going to betray the trust of an innocent maiden.

HONORIA: The Prince's face was a picture.

LAVINIA: Yes: A Stag At Bay. What could he do? You don't throw away a kingdom lightly, and he either had to do that or marry Cinderella.

PRESSMAN: So the fabulous Ball never really took place?

LAVINIA: Oh, yes, it did. Shall I ever forget that night!

HONORIA: Cinderella's Engagement Ball, it was. The high-spot was her speech.

LAVINIA: Yes, she actually had the impudence to tell them that idiotic dream of hers about pumpkins and mice and things, and how it had all come true, and – do you know —

PRESSMAN: – I know. Before you could look round, everyone believed it had really happened.

LAVINIA: Yes: how did you guess?

PRESSMAN: I've been a journalist for thirty years. I know what people will believe. What became of you two?

HONORIA: We were commanded by the Queen, our stepsister, to live in the Palace. An act of regal forgiveness, said the papers. She didn't want us out of her sight.

PRESSMAN: And the Godmother?

HONORIA: Ah, she died soon afterwards. She was poisoned. (*Pause.*) She knew too much, you know.

PRESSMAN (*appalled*): Good God!

The telephone rings.

HONORIA: Hallo? Yes, he's here. Hold on, please. It's for you.

PRESSMAN (*taking phone*): Thank you. I can't get over the cruelty of making you live in the same house with the man you loved.

LAVINIA: It may be that Cinderella made a mistake in doing that. The Prince was very much in love with me, you know. Always was. Do answer that phone, now – it's your paper. Tell them the truth. Goodbye.

HONORIA: Goodbye.

PRESSMAN: Goodbye, ladies, and thank you very much. (*Exeunt* SISTERS.) Hallo? . . . Yes, speaking . . . Who? The editor? . . . No, sir, I haven't got my interview yet . . . Well, I'm sorry, but I can't tell the Queen to get a move on, can I? . . . Have I anything to give you to get on with? Yes, enough to send us to war with Sudonia, I should think. That business about the mice turning into horses – seems to be phoney, after all. I've always had my doubts, haven't you? Well, look: briefly: Cinderella has been debunked. *She* was the ugly sister, not the other two. One of the sisters seems to have been the late King's mistress, by the way. How's that to be getting on with? . . . What? Oh, I see. We dare not print anything controversial. You want the usual legend plus trimmings . . . Yes, I understand. Best to be on the safe side . . .

Enter SECRETARY.

Just one moment, sir.

SECRETARY: Her Majesty will see you now.

PRESSMAN: Thank you very much. (*Into phone.*) Well, I'm going to see the Queen now . . . Yes, as soon as I can. The old sweet story . . . Nothing altered. Very good, sir . . . Yes . . . yes, sir . . . Yes. Goodbye for now. (*Replaces phone.*)

Lead on, ma'am. I am ready to be enchanted.

They go out as the CURTAIN *falls.*

Production Notes

MAKE YOUR PLAY

This is a burlesque version of the eternal Western. It will be noticed that, while the characters in the other plays all have appropriate names, only one is named here – Martha. The others are simply labelled – Old Timer, Sheriff, Bad Man, etc. They have – deliberately, of course – been taken from stock; they turn up in all the Westerns. The humour is derived from exaggerating the cliché situations in which such characters are involved.

The circumstances of Martha and the Old Timer are not stated exactly, but we gather that they make money out of telling Western yarns to tourists, who in this case are the audience. The Old Timer is as it were hypnotized by his own drawl, and carries on without a change of tone no matter how outrageous the plot becomes. Martha, shrill and exasperated, tries to make him stick to the point and give the audience their money's worth; but he ambles on, telling the wrong story, to its absurd happy ending.

Martha, despite her few lines, is important. She should speak twice as quickly as the other players, from whom she stands apart, and she should make her final speech at hysterical pitch. All should exaggerate the Western accent as much as possible – a comic accent is good for laughs for its own sake, and the producer should make sure that this is carefully practised.

The whole play should be acted 'straight'; the actors should take themselves seriously, no matter into what mess the Old Timer's bungled narrative gets them. It is his fault, not theirs.

In all Westerns, no matter how 'corny', the physical action is done to perfection. It is imperative that the action here, especially the gunfight, should be rehearsed until it is quite smooth, and looks spontaneous.

The play should be acted with gusto and the pace should be

brisk, although the Sheriff and the Saloon Girl should intersperse the lines of their brief love scene with some lingering by-play, or the audience may find this latest development too abrupt to comprehend.

No Western is complete without its background music, and the producer may care to record on tape some passages from actual Westerns, which could be usefully relayed during the play – just before the entry of the 'three mean-looking jaspers', for instance, and when the Sheriff and the Saloon Girl make their exit.

BRING OUT YOUR DEAD

This makes merry at the expense of hospital drama, with its discipline and its tension, its white coats, its medical jargon, its crises in the operating theatre, and its fascinating insight on the personal drama that goes on behind this routine. Several old friends turn up: the sardonic old surgeon with a heart of gold, the sensitive junior surgeon, the pretty little nurse, the spinster Sister past her youth, the taciturn anaesthetist. Writers of these scripts have limitless scope for characterization; any type can be introduced into a hospital story, and the odder the better. So we meet Dr Smirke, with his distorted echoes of T. S. Eliot, and Dr Fobia, with his peculiar English. Characterization is no less important here than in the original 'soap opera' of which it is a parody.

The Characters

All the characters should have a touch of caricature. MR MANDRAKE, arrogant, sardonic, imperious, has, of course, a shy craving for affection; we have a glimpse of this in his scene with Sister Hagbird. We suspect that he really thinks a terrific lot of young Malady, for all his biting sarcasm; and in the end, he shows that he does indeed, until the awful whereabouts of his missing teeth is discovered.

MR MALADY should be a dark genius, self-dramatizing, sorry for himself and rather spoilt. The joke is on him in this play, but the actor should not make him entirely unsympathetic. If the audience can feel sorry for him, as well as laugh at him, so much the better. The little scene with Nurse Poppet, for instance, should have its leavening of tenderness; the joke will be none the worse for that.

SISTER HAGBIRD should not be too forbidding. She is the best of the bunch; she sees through them all, except when blinded by her affection for Mr Malady. Although part of the play, she is a detached observer of the others, too; a critical guide for Dr Fobia.

DR FOBIA should be serpentine and graceful, with much flashing of white teeth and waving of the hands. His 'indeterminate race' is probably Indian.

DR SMIRKE should be bright and ingenuous, except when pronouncing his impressive diagnosis on Mr Mandrake, which should be spoken tersely, with an air of deep significance.

DR WALLABY should be as brashly 'Austr-eye-lian' as possible; the actor must take care to study the accent.

NURSE POPPET should be big-eyed and enraptured: the embodiment of a schoolgirl crush.

The actors should take themselves not only seriously, but just a little too seriously. The whole thing should be slightly overdone: the tenseness in the operating scenes a bit too tense, Nurse Poppet's adoration for Malady, and his 'bony, sensitive hands' just a little too adoring. Remember that the dramatic, overdone, becomes the absurd – and that is what we are aiming at.

I'LL RING FOR MORE TOAST

The producer must avoid treating this play merely as 'crazy comedy'. Although the behaviour of all the characters is more than far-fetched, it has point; the humour resides in everyone's rigid resistance to change. Mrs Swayne expects to be provided with toast, even though revolution is raging round her doors; Betty cannot see the point of marrying; Charles wants to play tennis in the rain; the Reds murder each other because they cannot agree about a point of policy. On the other hand, the play must not be treated as social satire. The middle classes have been the target for too much satire already, and this, rather, is a parody of it. It is not in itself satire; the fun is without rancour. We should laugh at these people amiably, even affectionately.

One must be well over forty to remember the early 'thirties, but there is no lack of reference. One of the best sources is *Punch*, and the producer is strongly recommended to get hold of some copies of that time. Their pictorial jokes will show him the dress and hair styles of the period, and show the make-up man what effect to aim at. The articles and stories will convey the atmosphere of the era, concerning which it might also help to read some of John Betjeman's 'suburban' poems, like 'a Subaltern's Love-Song'.

Careful attention must be paid to accent. The Swaynes, Charles and Lady Footle must have 'upper-class', Southern English accents. These should not be guyed; a music-hall 'la-di-da' accent would be quite wrong here The Reds should speak correctly. but harshly: they must 'rap', as the popular novelists put it.

The Characters
LADY FOOTLE. Vague, elegant, and extremely refined. She does

not lose decorum even at gun-point. The revolution, like the existence of the poor, is to her in extremely bad taste.

MRS SWAYNE. The revolution is simply not to be taken seriously; neither is Charles; nor is the report of her husband's death. Unpleasantness of any kind is overcome by maintaining that it simply doesn't exist. She is not vague, like Lady Footle; she is alert and supremely confident. Her manner should be consciously 'gracious', except when speaking to Charles, with whom she is blunt and impatient.

RUBBISH is a Jeevesian character, pompous, stout, very dignified. He moves majestically, and speaks with lordly resignation.

BETTY. Going to be exactly like her mother, but at present an ingenue, bouncing and rather hearty.

CHARLES. A 'genial ass' of a type very prevalent in the comedy of the period. The author has pushed him further up the scale of caricature than these originals, but he should not be a music-hall 'dude'. Charles suffers in this play, this way and that, and he must be likeable in his absurdity.

THE REDS. Dark, sallow, lean and starved-looking. Black suits and white shirts. Black, square-toed boots. Scarlet ties.

Stage Effects

Thunder is made by shaking a large sheet of tin; lightning by arrangement with the electrician. The sound of pouring rain can be produced by shaking grains of rice in a large tin box. Some advisers have suggested that real water should be sprinkled over Charles from a hose manipulated by Daddy, sitting on top of a flight of steps by his window; but this is rather hard on Charles, and besides could make such a mess as to make the cast very unpopular with the caretaker. Charles should wet his hair and assume a drenched attitude; the appearance of rain may be given to his clothes by sprinkling them with tiny pieces of tinsel, such as is used on Christmas trees.

Daddy's window presents no difficulties. He should be able to 'switch himself on', and it is advisable for him to have a small curtain to drop over his window, so that there is no sign of him during the rest of the play.

IS HORROR YOUR NEIGHBOUR?

A four-minute sketch of this kind goes down well at a concert, or as 'comic relief' between two serious one-acters. The acting should be exuberant and 'hammy' in the style associated with old-fashioned melodrama. The attendant should be heavily lugubrious in tone; the visitor's mounting terror may be conveyed by extravagant mime, as in an old silent film; the wax models should chant their lines with evil glee, 'Nellie Dean' should be an exultant yell, and the ensuing dance-and-cackle may be as abandoned as they can make it without injuring themselves.

When the attendant returns with his bottle of 'Nervo', the voices of all, in contrast, should become fatuously over-friendly, and Jane the Ripper should recite her little speech in an excessively ingratiating tone. It is impossible to overdo this; the advertisements on television provide the actors with more than enough examples.

This sketch is quite straightforward and allows young actors to let off steam, but careful rehearsal of poses and movements is essential. Indeed, more rehearsal is needed for this kind of thing, length for length, than for a serious play. A ragged or clumsy skit is inexcusable. Much the same preparation is required as would be given to a dancing display. Fortunately, so short a piece may be run through several times in a single rehearsal.

A VILLA ON VENUS

We members of the Human Race do not show up well in this light-hearted satire. We are the backward boys of the Solar System, arrogant, stupid, and addicted to destruction. The Venusians, a much more intelligent lot, are correspondingly decent. Sham and Gimble want nothing so much as to help others and make them happy. The Earthmen set them a problem, which the Mercurian salesman, Spiv, helps them, providentially, to solve. And if blowing the Earth to pieces is rather drastic, it seems to be what the Earthmen want; it makes a fortune for Spiv, and it prevents the spread of earthly villas across Venus, which even the Bug-Eyed Monsters deem more than they can bear.

This play may be considered to fall into the following sections:

1. Up to the arrival of the Earthmen. Sham and Gimble should establish themselves as excellent chaps, the product of centuries of enlightenment. This opening scene makes it clear that we are seeing all through Venusian eyes, and that Earthmen, thus seen, are not welcome visitors.

2. From the arrival of Frank Fearless and his friends to the entry of the Bug-Eyed Monsters. The actors should try to make the Earthmen likeable in their stupidity. They are not so much villains as unconscious comedians, deaf to the subtleties of Sham ('I'm afraid life's rather like the cheapest fiction, my boy') and an easy prey for the Bug-Eyed Monsters. They shock the youthful Gimble, but Sham, older and wiser, is unsurprised. His only problem is how to entertain them.

3. The scene with the Bug-Eyed Monsters. These must be bloodthirsty and repulsive, in order to bring out the contrast in their later scene, when they reveal that the Earthmen shock

even their sense of propriety. They must be comically diabolical, however. Their howls of fiendish glee – 'Murder and death!' must be pure burlesque.

4. The scene with Spiv, who should be a disappointed little person, a humble inferior of the Venusians, who treat him most kindly. This little scene is quiet, in contrast to the boisterous one preceding it. It is even possible to extract a little pathos from it. Gimble's 'Poor old Spiv' is spoken with genuine concern.

5. The return of the Bug-Eyed Monsters, with their horrid revelations of Earthly life. They are abject and grovelling, and, we realize, not so bad after all; not so bad as we are, anyway. Sham's disgust should not be in the least ill-natured. He keeps them at a distance rather as we might a dog who had just emerged from a muddy ditch.

6. The final scene between the Earthmen and Spiv. Their admiration for him, when they learn of his remarkable range of products, should be like that of public schoolboys for some cricketing hero. They are, as characters, indistinguishable one from the other – their schoolboy-fiction names could easily be swopped around – they are more like old Empire-builders than modern space-travellers.

Costumes

Designers of futuristic Utopias are pretty much agreed about dress; the best people all dress like Ancient Greeks, and Sham and Gimble should be no exception to this, in tasteful knee-length *chitons*. Spiv should dress similarly, with the addition of a shabby cloak. The Earthmen should wear form-fitting 'space-suits' which emphasize the muscular male underneath. The Bug-Eyed Monsters may follow whatever is the latest trend in Things, although the perambulating milk-churns of a current vogue are to be avoided. Black tights with the bones of the skeleton picked out on them are suggested, and goggles fixed to resemble huge yellow eyes.

YOU NEVER HEARD SUCH UNEARTHLY LAUGHTER

Snobbery affronted by vulgarity has provided many an author with a comic theme. Here the snobs are ghosts, and the vulgarians are thrust upon them for all eternity. There are intimations, however, that the younger ghosts won't find the new company so bad.

The play progresses from polite comedy to slapstick. The formalities of life in the castle are broken by the arrival of the awful newcomers, and the ghosts, when we see them again, are shaken out of their complacency. The next scene, where they make their too-successful attempt to frighten the Higgins family, should be uproarious, and will repay careful working over in rehearsal. The last scene, as the dreadful truth dawns on the Duchess, is deliberate anticlimax. This play has 'a sting in its tail', and the Duchess must take care not to throw away the last line, which should be uttered ringingly and with deliberation.

Both families are familiar ones in English comedy. The ghosts' standards of correct behaviour are set by the mother, domineering and statuesque; the father is her staunch ally, with some old-fashioned grumbles of his own; the children are on the whole acquiescent, but show some faint sparks of rebellion. The Higgins family are readily recognizable as 'a common lot'. The author has made them Cockneys, but there is no need to stick to this; the accent of the local plebs, wherever the play is produced, will suit them admirably.

The producer should take care that neither the disdain of the ghosts nor the vulgarity of the Higginses is unpleasant. We should like each group, and enjoy their antics. The Duchess may be 'an old battle-axe', but she should win our regard for her sporting spirit; her husband is genial in a 'Blimpish' way; Geoffroy has boyish charm and Matilda is a nice little thing with an innocent love of mischief. The outrageous Higginses have plenty of vitality, except for the plaintive Ma, who is a good foil for the others.

Green spotlight should be directed on the Higginses when they awake from their swoon, to give them the pallor appropriate to their new state. 'Ghostly' make-up, of course, is needed for the ghosts, but its consistency will depend largely on the kind of lighting in use.

This is the tale of Cinderella from the viewpoint of the Ugly Sisters, and everything is seen in a different light. The sisters were really nice girls, Cinderella was a little beast, the stepmother was a good sort and the Fairy Godmother an interfering old trouble-maker. The author felt that this would make a change from letting Cinderella win every pantomime, and that it might be refreshing, for once, for the Prince to be a boy and the Ugly Sisters girls.

The first hint that there are flaws in the legend is found in the guarded speeches of the Secretary. Our suspicions are confirmed on the entrances of Lavinia and Honoria. These two are import-ant; much of the success of the play depends on how well they can bring conviction and animation to speeches which (especially in the Epilogue) are mainly explanatory. There is also the problem of their ages. Probably the actresses playing these parts will not find it difficult to portray young girls, but they may find it harder to represent the age of seventy. The sisters in age are far from doddery or senile; they are spirited and alert, and we should be able to see that when young they were exceedingly attractive. But they must talk and move at a more measured rate than they do in youth. An occasional slight stiffness of movement, a hesita-tion or deliberation in their speech, will suggest elderliness, and make the sudden change to youth more effective. At twenty, Honoria should be attractively tomboyish, rather 'jolly' in manner, and Lavinia a feminine, delightful girl, a young man's ideal.

Cinderella is a type known to all of us; she contrives to put everyone but herself in the wrong. A mischievous, unprincipled little minx rather than a neurotic, she is shrewd enough to pretend to be a neurotic to the Prince; in fact she knows just what face to present to everyone, except the family, who see through her. This is not an easy part to play. We must be aware all the time that she is *an actress*, slipping from part to part: wistful and pathetic with her Godmother, frank and worried before the Prince, and so on; her only completely sincere line is 'And don't bungle it, you old cow', which is said when she is alone.

The Prince is a good fellow, but, as he admits himself, not too bright. Patient with Cinderella at first through sheer good manners, he allows himself to become interested in her 'case' and is then quickly snared.

The Godmother is one of those tiresome people who fight crusades where none is called for, and think themselves better than everyone else for doing so. Perhaps jealousy of the Baroness's happy, healthy family makes her side with Cinderella.

The producer may decide that this play satirizes the way the Press distorts the truth for the sake of cheap, sentimental sensation. The final speech of the honest Pressman might seem to bear this out. But he must not forget that it is farce, and must be played briskly, for laughs. Just as we take lightly the sufferings of the original Cinderella, so we should take lightly the machinations and duplicity of this one. A solemn Cinderella is out of the question, whichever side we are on.